Stop
Pouring Out Your Power

The End of People-Pleasing —
Becoming Untamed

Rachel Piccoli

DISCLAIMER

The information in this book is intended for educational and entertainment purposes only.

This book is not intended to be a substitute for legal, medical, psychological, or professional advice. The author and publisher are not offering professional advice.

The author, publisher and editor (Sekinat Taiwo) assumes no responsibility for your actions and specifically disclaims responsibility for any liability, loss, risk, or any physical, psychological, emotional, or financial damages, personal or otherwise, which is incurred as a consequence, directly or indirectly, of the use and application of any of the contents of this book.

Stop Pouring Out Your Power/Rachel Piccoli - 1st ed.

LCCN: 2026900064
ISBN: 979-8-9944432-5-5 (Hardback)
ISBN: 979-8-9944432-2-4 (Ebook)
ISBN: 979-8-9944432-4-8 (Paperback)

TABLE OF CONTENT

SECTION THREE: UNTAMED

DEDICATION

For Gracie—your words matter. Your soul matters. The world is better because you are in it. I love you to Infinity.

For Grace, Carlene, Mary Jayne, Linda, and the women who came before me—whose names I carry in my blood, whose strength lives in my bones—and for the women who will come after me.

May this book be a remembering, a return, a gift to walk freer because of what we dared to heal.

PREFACE

*I*t is hard to evaluate all the mistakes or mishaps that have happened in one's life, to wrap it up into a book and send it out into the world for others to interpret.

This book poured from my heart as a divine gift to you— a gift to help you see how much of yourself you have given away, pleasing others. Life is a rare and precious experience that shapes every person into who they are through their realities and upbringing. It is a true miracle to be a soul having this human adventure.

I have a few stories and experiences to share in this book. The goal is to connect them with lessons and questions that resonate with you. Please take a moment to reflect on your own life with each question and evaluate how people-pleasing relates to you or how it could be holding you back.

Years ago, I finally saw how it held me back. I could trace my 'people-pleasing' mentality to my upbringing and my experiences of the world. I grew up in the most loving family—one could ask for—parents and a brother. They have always been there for me, cheering me on and supporting me entirely, and I love them dearly. I'm not sharing these stories to blame anyone; I'm sharing them because they're part of the journey that made me who I am today.

I was meant to go through the following experiences to learn, grow, and break free from them. I was meant to be a guide for you in the realm of healing and growth, helping you break generational patterns that came down through your lineage.

PREFACE

This book is a first step. For those ready to go deeper, there are tools and exercises to help you fully reclaim your power—but that comes after you've reflected on your own journey. Along the way, you'll reflect on your patterns, face your fears, and start reclaiming the energy, confidence, and joy that belong to you. Everything changes once you change. Patterns are interrupted, deep relationships are connected, you become the person you have always felt you've been inside, yet have trembled at the prospect of becoming her, and you even end up pouring your medicine out to the world, getting to light it up.

Like wild horses that have been locked up for years, there is a rumble in your heart, essence, and soul. This book is the gate unlatching, so you might escape from performing and instead run wild, free, and unapologetic towards your passion—Untamed.

Inviting you to unlace your good girl skin,

Rachel Piccoli

Section ONE

SHACKLED

People Pleaser:

"A person who has an emotional need to please others at the expense of his or her own needs or desires."

CHAPTER 1
HELLO, MEET YOUR PLEASER

*I*t seems like two lifetimes ago that I found myself sitting on a green couch in a small, ten-by-ten office, staring at a calm, clean-lined psychologist who would say one sentence that would shift my life. A sentence that would change the paradigm I was living in. I wasn't in crisis; nobody was sick or dying. But mentally, I was exhausted.

I had been referred to her by a naturopath for adrenal fatigue— complete exhaustion, sleepless nights, and a body that felt like it carried the world and wasn't mine. The naturopath suspected I was holding a lot more emotionally than I needed to, and this doctor—an EMDR expert—would help me process trauma and cleanse me from PTSD.

Now, I didn't think I had PTSD, but I had a memory of a horse accident a year and a half prior. This awful memory was trapped inside my muscles and was causing my nervous system to overreact and my mind to be on edge all the time.

If you are a mother, you can relate that it comes naturally to overthink. When you add trauma stuck in the muscles and neuropathways, it creates a person within you that you don't recognize: a mom who wants to nap on the couch, having never made it into a deep sleep at night. A mom who couldn't peel herself off that couch in the afternoons to play with her toddler, who was so delightfully fun. A mom who was getting uptight and fearful of events that she had never been bothered by, a mom who became the "be careful mom" saying it every time her daughter barely got close to the edge of something unsafe, and at every slight jerk in a car as a passenger, my nervous system would send tiny little pin needles through my fingers and toes. Sure, maybe it was true that I needed some help with PTSD, so I went. At that point, I was tired and frustrated with all the symptoms that were making me feel less and less like myself.

We had a few sessions before the revelation that changed my life. I was becoming more relaxed and comfortable in my own body than I had been in the year prior. The EMDR was working beautifully to release the stored emotions in my body and rewire the memory to be just that, a memory, not a trauma.

This session was different; I was carrying pent-up frustration from a lifetime of misunderstandings and wrongdoings with a particular family member. It weighed heavily on my heart, and it was beginning to turn into anger. That is when she said the epiphany sentence —the one that was a mental shift and would change how I viewed life. She had a confused look on her face as I was processing what she had said. A look I envisioned as though a human were trying to explain gravity to a non-earth dweller. My eyebrows were scrunched, my lip was up, and my nose wrinkled. I said, "Huh? Can you repeat that?" So she did. "Just because they are family doesn't mean you have to be around them," she stated slowly, questioning why I was confused.

With that one sentence, she rocked my world.

I grew up in a family that owned a business together and had been taught my entire life: even if you don't want to be in the same room with someone, you show up. You show up to every family event, put on a "I'm not bothered" yet "I am not speaking to you" face. I was shown that family is the most important thing on this earth, so even if you don't like one of them, you get together anyway.

When the psychologist's words flew out of her mouth like she was saying "I'm going to the store"—so casually—I was confused. You might also be sitting there, confused—not thinking this is a life-transforming sentence —but for this trained people pleaser, it rocked my world. In what world is it okay to say 'no' when you don't want to be around someone, especially a family member? I was 32 at the time, and this mindset was still running strong through my blood like a herd of wild horses; strong and not stopping any moment soon.

When we continued speaking specifically about the recent encounter with this family member, I explained to her that I had tried to work with this person in the past. Still, it always seemed to end with me walking away feeling like crap about myself. She went on to explain the word "boundary" as a place where I don't have to invite this person into my life. What? I felt my face relax and what felt like years of "have to's" dissolve into that couch. Let me take you back to the generations that shaped me.

My grandma was an earthly angel, someone who had beauty and grace and left this earth too young due to being a part of the generation that started smoking. She was a tiny little lady with black raven hair and a fair, stunning complexion. At some point in her life, she was referred to as a young Elizabeth Taylor.

She married my grandpa, and they had two boys and a girl, my mom. My grandma was one of the most generous and kind-hearted women—a true angel in disguise—who came with the side effect of helping people less fortunate. She would give them rides, bring them home for dinner, and even wanted to have them stay the night, but my grandpa put his foot down and told her no to hosting slumber parties. She was so shy, but her heart and actions showed her love for people. She was a true empath and a possible people-pleaser, trapped in her own body and mind. My mother watched her unbelievably talented and shy mom repeatedly serve others before her own family and self. She was so severely introverted that she would often send my mom into stores where she didn't want to socialize. When she was comfortable, she would reveal her prominent personality, showing her beautiful, creative talents, such as dancing and playing the piano. She was full of happiness and delight, wrapped in humor, but bottled up by the restrictions and fears of her introversion.

My mom inherited the same pattern—serving others before herself—though she wore it differently. Where my grandma was introverted, my mom was outgoing, proving her worth by keeping up with the men in her family and giving endlessly to those around her. A beautiful gift, when balanced. Destructive, when not.

When my parents married, my mom wanted to help with the family business's bookkeeping. But "helping" turned into "taking over" when my grandma was diagnosed with emphysema from years of smoking. She died at 58. I was in elementary school.

My mom didn't get time to grieve. She was the only one who could step into that accounting seat, so she did—learning the job while burying her best friend.

She would leave the house as we got on the bus and would not be home until midnight. She was working so hard and was exhausted, but never felt she could say, "No, I need a break." Before all of this happened, my parents had built their own house; my brother and I relied on the acreage we lived on and our imaginations to entertain ourselves. The demand for her job lasted for years; she is a hard worker, and her integrity sets the tone. The piles of work had her missing some events my brother and I were involved in; however, she always threw a "mean" birthday party full of creativity, making us feel like we were the most important beings. She wasn't absent by any means, but her missing presence was noticed. She and my dad were doing what they had to do to contribute to the lifestyle my brother and I were privileged to grow up in. We got to do activities that weren't cheap, but my parents knew it was important to us, so they made it work. The electricity was always on, and food was always available. Yet there was a looming heaviness of co-dependency deeply embedded in my mom, with a pinch or two of people pleasing all wrapped in a tight little "small town" package.

This package was sprinkled with cliques and gossiping gals who really emphasized the people-pleaser within— if you have ever lived in a small town, you know what I am talking about. It's not until you move away that you really understand how big the world is and shed the piece of you that might care about what Jennie down the street thinks of your outfit of the day and other nonsense she spreads.

Back to the word co-dependency: my mother—one of my best friends—a badass—an absolute excellent, high-energy, people-loving, kickass businesswoman, had it deeply rooted in her, which, in turn, shaped my interactions with other humans, often ending with a talk about what I might have said right or wrong. I got very used to being gently graded for the tone or words I used that might have made the other person feel uneasy.

Each time we had these talks, I sank deeper and deeper into not knowing who I was or if I was safe when I spoke. I started holding back what I really wanted to say, even when those words wanted to come barreling out of my mouth. It was painful; it felt as though a piece of me was dying —a piece that knew my own likes and dislikes. It felt as though I was wrong and not enough.

This pain slowly turned to feeling numb, as I learned to be the "good little girl" and not rock anybody's boat with my personal opinion. Following the breadcrumbs of the generations before me, I see how she genuinely thought it was making me a better person and giving me deeper people skills by correcting much of what I said. At 32, I was now a full-fledged people pleaser, watching the subtle cues of others' body language and ebbing when they flowed and flowing when they ebbed. The problem was that the people pleaser within me was making me sick. I worried about everything, and if there were a slightly offbeat encounter, I would hold on to it for days, weeks, and sometimes years. I became the dependable one.

The thing about being the dependable one is that it makes you feel noble at first, until you realize you're slowly becoming invisible. You forget what you want, like, or feel; your intuition is silent, yet your mind races constantly. You swallow up your disappointments and your voice. Your true self, soul's purpose, and heart's desires become so distant that you can no longer hear them.

Here I was, a fully grown woman, realizing I was tired of living for others. I began replaying specific conversations, wondering why I had agreed to things I didn't want and why I had never spoken up in certain situations.

I even felt guilty for imagining my opinions mattered, and my chest beat faster when I wanted to speak up, only to deny myself and remain quiet.

Sitting on this psychologist's couch was a huge turning point and awakening for me, a moment I realized how shackled by my thoughts I had become. I began to pay attention to the parts of me I had ignored for years. **The way People Pleasing can show up:**

The Self Sacrificer – Constantly putting the needs of others before their own.

Approval Seeker – Deep drive to be liked and approved by others.

Overly Responsible/Performer – They take on too much to receive praise and are fueled by that praise.

Indecisive/Martyr — Not being able to choose for fear of choosing the "incorrect" option.

Fear of conflict/Chameleon – Feeling of unsafety when someone doesn't agree with your opinion.

Good little girl/boy – Rests most of their confidence on how they perform and on whether they get approval from others.

Peacemakers – They are unnerved when you are upset with them and will self-sacrifice to keep the peace, even when it costs them.

The Sorry – Apologizing for EVERYTHING – "I am sorry it's taking me so long to fill up my water bottle."

The Fixer – Similar to the peacemaker, but will go out of their way to feel like they need to fix a problem for someone outside of them, even a coworker who fought with a spouse. They take that problem on as if it were their own.

Emotionally numb – Runs from thing to thing, over-scheduling and complicating to not actually stop and face what is chasing them, it's too scary, they can't process it.

The giver/over helper – They typically go above and beyond, making gestures beyond the norm and sometimes making it awkward for the other person, or giving in a way the other person didn't actually want.

The loyalist — They need connection and security through being with that person; they avoid being alone.

The silent agreer – Avoids being vulnerable or judged, perhaps, nods and or always agrees even when they don't actually agree.

These behaviors can appear one at a time or in waves. Some may feel familiar to you, while others may not fit at all—and that's okay.

A Self-Assessment Exercise

This book is meant to give you my awkward, vulnerable stories — what I went through — and to demonstrate some of the people-pleasing ways that showed up in my journey. In my life, I have experienced all of these behaviors.

Your turn. Do take a moment to place these traits into the three categories below. Be honest and kind with yourself as you reflect.
Also, tag them with a specific person or situation that happens when they appear.
(Use a journal or notebook to write your responses if you prefer not to write in this book.)

1.   Traits that show up the most (daily, weekly, monthly)
(These are your strongest patterns and often the hardest to break.)

2.   Traits that show up sometimes (monthly or a few times a year):
(Present, but less intense)

3.   Traits that show up rarely (once or twice a year)
(Usually appearing when you're stressed, overwhelmed, or emotionally vulnerable.)

Why This Matters

"Fear is the Gateway to Confidence" – Rachel Piccoli

Everything you've listed in category one will require the most attention and honesty from you. Category two patterns are easier to shift, and category three often fades naturally once the root is addressed.

You can start wherever feels safest, but don't avoid the hard ones. Growth happens when we face the fear behind our patterns, not when we work only on what feels comfortable.

You are the gatekeeper to all your desires; you decide if you lock yourself up or spread your wings. Until you understand this, you will continue to blame others.
You, my love, will go as far as you open your heart and mind.

Moving Forward

This chapter was your introduction to the people pleaser living inside you. Now that you've met her, felt her impact, and recognized the pieces of your true self that have gone missing, I invite you to turn the page.

Because next, we'll trace the threads that led you away from yourself—so you can learn to weave yourself back together.

Trust me, my love. The journey ahead will feel empowering, wildly freeing, terrifying, and bitchy all at once.

CHAPTER 2
YOU ARE NOT GUMBY

Suppose you have pegged yourself as a people pleaser. You've done the work from Chapter 1 and identified your strongest patterns. Most likely, it was a slow accumulation of habits over time—small movements—like watching grass grow every day, subtle, but, over time, significant and unruly.

You are not a bad person.

Hear me again, my love: you are not a bad person. You have not done anything wrong. Let's clear this up right now.

The "Energy Vampire" Myth

There are all kinds of opinions out in the world, and some are now labeling people pleasers as energy vampires. Let's be real—What the heck, really?
I am not sure those people have been around a true people pleaser, because they don't suck your energy. They are ready to serve, eager to care about you, your feelings, and your well-being. Some might be people pleasers with an extra dash of obsession or even deep insecurities that drive an unhealthy attachment to you, which could be smothering. But most people pleasers will make you feel like the most important person. You will be so loved and supported.

However, I am going to say the thing you will not want to hear:

THIS WAS NEVER YOUR INTENTION, but people-pleasing is a form of manipulation.

Take a breath. I know that hits hard and sucks.

As a recovered people pleaser, manipulation was the opposite of what I ever desired or wanted for the other person. When I first heard this, it felt like someone slapped me, ripped out the rug, and threw me in a jail cell—everything I had ever gone above and beyond for was done manipulatively? Gasp. Eyes wide open at the horror.

Once I took a breath and reminded my heart to open up again and hear this woman's perspective, I could understand how she would reach that conclusion.

The People Pleaser's Reality

You see, when you are a people pleaser, you are not being authentically you. You ebb and flow to serve the other person better, thereby subconsciously manipulating how that person perceives you.

I know it sucks. I personally know other people pleasers, and they are the biggest-hearted, palms-wide-open, ready-to-serve-anyone-who-needs-help kind of souls. Their intention has never been, and will never be, a selfish act. Quite the opposite, actually—they have a problem with overserving and neglecting themselves.

They run ragged. They have the inflatable balloon hand, which is ridden with guilt if it doesn't get raised, even if it means adding another task to their already-overloaded schedule. They give all they have, and even after that, feel guilt for something done incorrectly or for not being able to provide more.

Small stuff? Medium stuff? Large stuff? If it's stuff, they're worried about it and confuse others in their life about why they were so bothered by a tiny incident. The little things they might say or do wrong make them spin until they run themselves right into an autoimmune disease.

They pride themselves on doing a job well done and work harder when praised—which is so dangerous and a clear pathway to attracting a predator personality that actually loves to use people for what they can get out of them.

It is typically the people pleasers who end up in horrible relationships because they have a weak spine. Yes, I said it. I don't mean it meanly—I mean it compassionately, as I've lived this myself. They can easily end up dating the wrong people who take advantage of them repeatedly and possibly abuse them emotionally or even physically. Still, the people pleaser stays because they are, sadly and sincerely, desiring to be loved and accepted.

Where It All Begins

They didn't learn to self-regulate well as kids. They didn't know that it's okay to have their own opinion without being told it's wrong. They didn't understand that if they mess up, they are still loved no matter what.
They can also come from a home that has an unstable parent or caregiver. It creates a behavior of tiptoeing around, trying not to rock the boat, because when they do, the results are terrifying. They find themselves hiding in a closet until it ends, being abused in some form, and shown they are not loved or valued.

Babies are not born as people pleasers.

It is a learned coping mechanism to keep everybody in their lives happy—for safety, or to feel connected, cherished, loved, and enough just the way they are. They are not intentionally being manipulative. They are coping to maintain homeostasis in their bodies and minds.

They don't think they are harming you or being disingenuous. Most of them will be shocked after years of pouring their souls out to find that what they are doing is a form of manipulation, and they will be so hurt that it could be taken that way.

Your Freeing Truth

My goal for you, if you are currently a people pleaser, is to be open to the freeing possibilities that will arise when you learn, accept, and embody this deep knowing:

You are the only one who can determine your worth and value.

Not because you worked harder or said and did all the perfectly perfect things, but because you know your own soul—and it is filled with integrity, care, love, joy, hope, and badassery that has been dying to be let out and freed.

It is up to you to let her out.
She has been hidden away for too long—so long you might be nervous to unleash her in fear of what she might do and the "I don't give a crap" attitude she might reveal.

The Lesson

Here's the truth: it doesn't matter how much you bend over backward for someone in this lifetime. They could still misinterpret what you're doing from their perspective. They might see it as a bad thing, manipulation, or neediness—no matter how pure your intentions.

So start doing things that light you up.

When you are lit up, your whole environment will feel it. You will pour from your overflow instead of your empty cup. And that, my love, changes everything.

Now that you've sat with the uncomfortable truth of manipulation and understand where these patterns began, it's time to look inward. The questions below aren't meant to shame you—they're meant to free you.

Reflection Questions

Take some time to sit with these questions. Journal your responses. Be honest, raw, and kind with yourself.

1. **How does it make you feel when you hear that people-pleasing can be seen as manipulation or that people pleasers are labeled "energy vampires"?** Where does it land in your body? What emotions come up?

2. **Can you see how others outside of you might interpret your people-pleasing behavior that way, even though it's not your intention?** Instead of letting this spiral, what shifts when you consider their perspective?

3. **Could you release a small piece of needing to clarify your intentions to everyone?** Practice saying out loud: "I am not for everybody," and "I am safe learning to be clearer with what I desire and what my opinion is." How does that feel in your body?

4. **Where is the "good little girl" showing up in your life right now?** In what situations do you find yourself performing, over-explaining, or apologizing when you don't need to?

Remember: You are not Gumby. You don't have to bend and twist yourself into shapes that hurt just to make others comfortable. The real you—the one who's been hiding—is powerful, worthy, and ready to stop apologizing for taking up space.

CHAPTER 3
BORN WITH AUDACITY

Let's back it up a little. I have always been a social soul.

I grew up in a small town in the beautiful state of Colorado. When I was 6 months old, my parents—who had moved to Phoenix for a couple of years—decided to return home and to their family. They lived in a trailer park for a few months while trying to find a place in the countryside. They ended up finding a place down an old cul-de-sac lane and had their trailer moved out to those acres of land.

It was a small neighborhood with a few other houses nearby. My parents met some of their best friends on that lane, friends they're still close with today. We used to walk down to their house, and my parents would play cards until the wee hours of the morning while we kids played until we dropped on the couch, too tired to move another step.

We were familiar with where their home was in our new neighborhood.

I was about 3 years old at this time, and I didn't know a stranger. I wasn't shy, reserved, or fearful of anything—except maybe spiders. (Thank goodness I've gotten better with them since working in my flower gardens.)

One winter Saturday morning, my mom was home cleaning the house, vacuuming, and making noise. My brother was playing with his Hot Wheels cars. My dad was out back working on our family car.

I decided I wanted a cookie.

I didn't think my mom would allow me to have one, but I knew who would—my neighbor. They always had cookies and offered them to me so generously. I am a natural problem solver, so, of course, I decided to go down to my neighbor's house and get one.

I put on all the clothes I needed—a warm jacket, a hat, boots, and gloves—and stepped out into the cold, sunny day. It was longer than I remembered, and my feet started hurting from the hard snow on the ground. But I was determined to get what I wanted. The obstacle didn't matter.

Knock, knock, knock.

The door opened, and Richard—a very tall and slender man—stood in front of me. His eyes widened, and his voice shuddered with surprise. "Rachel, come in!" He was a kind man, so he took it in stride, though I could hear the alarm in his voice. "What are you doing here?"

"I was wondering if I could have a cookie," I replied.

A slight chuckle arose from his surprised demeanor. "I am sure we can make that happen. First, let's call your parents and let them know you're here." I shrugged my shoulders. "Ok, then can I have a cookie?"

"Yes, Rachel, then you can have a cookie," he said, I am sure with the look on his face, thinking, "She is crazy. What is happening? Why is the three-year-old alone?!"

Could we call it crazy? Yes. Or fearless, determined, and self-led to follow my desire, no matter what was in front of me!

Of course, a few minutes before Richard called, the reality that one of my mom's children was missing had set in. My mom had finally made it back to my room to vacuum and was confused when she didn't find me playing with my dollies.

She went looking and calling through the house, checking with my brother and dad, who confirmed they hadn't seen me. Her heart started to race. She could feel her breath grow both faster and shorter at the same time.

She threw on her coat with shaky hands, trying to zip it, when the phone rang.

She answered with a panicked "Hello." The sound of fear was rippling out of her throat.

It was Richard.

She didn't have time to talk to her friends—her mind was racing. The first words he spoke, upon hearing the panic in her voice, were "I have Rachel."

A burst of tears welled in her eyes, and a deep sigh escaped her lungs, even though just a second before, she had felt as though there was no air to breathe.

"I'm coming," is all she said as she hung up the phone and yelled to my dad, "I found her. I'll be back."

I don't remember the implications of my actions that day. I am sure we talked about how inappropriate it was to leave the house by myself at that age, especially without telling anyone.

As a parent, I can't imagine having a child who has no fear and bravely walks away from their home; I would be terrified, and I am grateful I didn't experience that.

And although it scared the shit out of my parents, I got what I desired.

Here's What This Means for You

This is going to—or maybe already has—happened in your life: when you follow your desires, sometimes it scares the shit out of the people around you.

Yes, leaving the house at three years old without my parents was wrong, and I was lucky it worked out in my favor. I am sure my divine guides were rolling their eyes, thinking, "Oh boy, this one is going to keep us on our toes."

With that being said, YOUR DESIRES are divine breadcrumbs that may not make sense to ANYONE but you.

You are not here to make all your dreams make sense to them. Your soul is here to do something that is only felt by you. You may have made choices in your life that don't make sense to others around you who care for you.

Sometimes you will feel like you are stepping into the dark because your soul keeps pulling you in a direction you don't feel qualified to go. You feel terrified—like you are standing alone and no one understands—yet you literally can't shake the pull. You may take a different route, but somehow the path keeps leading you back.

I am not talking about bad habits or addictions. I am talking about the dreamers—the people who have an inkling of thoughts that sound like, "Me? How could I do that? I am not qualified"—yet your soul knows you are, and perhaps it would be your life's biggest lesson and work.

The Lesson

We are born free—with inner audacity, with our power intact, and closest to the divine at that moment.

It can be said that your soul has a past life and may bring its own baggage. But much of the unnecessary baggage is taught to us through our upbringing and experiences, through generational teachings that keep coming down the line—whether they are good or need to be released. This pattern will continue as long as we are in human form, learning life lessons.

Reflection Questions

Think about the desires you've been pushing down. The dreams that light you up when you let yourself imagine them. Journal on these:

1. **What have you always wanted to do that your soul keeps lighting up about?** What direction keeps calling to you, even when you try to ignore it?

2. **Why have you held back?** Was it the influence of others? Or the fear of rising and breaking through, heart wide open, to the terrifying and magnifying purpose you've been keeping in the deep dark depths of your soul?

3. **What would happen if you followed those divine breadcrumbs?** You never know until you try.

CHAPTER 4
APPROVAL SEEKER

My three-year-old self knew what bravery and desire were without even thinking twice. She was completely embodied in them and unafraid of how they would affect others around her.

How We Learn to Dim Our Light.

As we get further into this human life, we learn through watching the loved ones around us and modeling or reacting to their behavior and influence. A baby comes into this world as a clean slate—a piece of clay ready to be molded and sculpted into a divine masterpiece of existence. Yet along the way, it also picks up undesirable generational or learned traits and bad habits as it grows and evolves.

We end up living in a state of constant reaction to life rather than seeing our specific world as a movie we can co-create.

There is no blame toward anyone for this happening. It is just a fact of life. Each generation learns from the previous one and, consciously or unconsciously, decides what it brings forward as an adult. Some behaviors are so subtle that you are not even aware that you are doing them. In contrast, others are behaviors you swore you would never do because you hated it when your parents did it—but they are now running strong in the adult version of yourself.

The "Convenience Friend"

Let's take it back again to see how life can influence someone's journey.

As a child in elementary school, there are a lot of pressures: trying to make new friends, learning all your required academics, mastering hopscotch at recess, and getting your clay mold to look like something other than a crinkly mess.

My brother is three years older than I, and he had already made friends by the time I started kindergarten. One of his friends also had a younger sister my age, so it was convenient for the parents to arrange playdates—ensuring both their sons and daughters would get to spend time together.

At first, this girlfriend was fun and funny. As time went on, her spice of life emerged, and it had a side of anger that my soul didn't understand. I was a young girl who just wanted to get along, have fun, and play.

When we would get together, she would beat up her older brother—wrestling with him, throwing punches, putting him in a headlock. I was giggling on the sidelines, but my eyes were wide with awe at how strong she was, and I was confused that this behavior was allowed in their house, as it would never be permitted in my own.

She was a powerhouse, full of piss and vinegar, which also made her funny and, mainly, fun to be around. But then there were the edges—the sharp edges—where the anger within her needed to be released, and whoever was the weakest link was the target.

The first time I can recall this happening was in second grade. I was over at her house for a playdate. I was in my own imaginary world, playing make-believe, dancing, dressing up in fancy clothes, and having tea. She didn't like something I did, so she left her room and locked me in it.

Yes, her locks were on the outside of her door—so maybe this had happened to her, and her make-believe was that I was the child who misbehaved and she was the parent.

Her room was always dark, with the shades pulled and clothes everywhere. She didn't like cleaning her room, which made it tricky to step anywhere without smashing toys or clothes. At seven years old, being locked in her room was alarming to me. I had never been locked in any room by myself, let alone a dark one that had a dim lava lamp light.

I tried to open the door, and it wouldn't budge. I hadn't even thought it was weird when she left the room and closed the door behind her because most of the time when we played, we had the door closed so the boys wouldn't bother us. Her mom was usually cleaning the house and doing laundry, so I am sure she couldn't hear what was going on for a while.

I don't know when or what made her decide to open the door and let me out, but it felt like eternity.

Something inside me panicked. I was knocking on the inside of the door, confused, as a feeling of being trapped and claustrophobia washed over me. I asked to be let out several times, getting louder and louder as it went on. It may have only been a minute or two, but at that age, it felt like eternity, and I was upset.

Why the heck would a friend want to lock another friend up, even at seven years old?

Once she opened the door, she just laughed when she saw the tears bubbling up in my eyes. It got downplayed, and I was supposed to move on and act like it wasn't a big deal, and it never happened.

This was the start of the ridiculously dumb and ornery friendship I experienced with her. We were living in a small town, in similar clubs, groups, and activities. Our brothers were friends, so again it was a convenient friendship that, looking back, should've never continued past that point.

Yet I still didn't learn my lesson.

By the time I reached sixth grade, she and one of her friends made up an elaborate story that some cute boy liked me and that they would talk to him about me and see if he wanted to chat. This boy lived in a neighboring town, so I didn't know him personally, but she described him as a guy a few of my friends had a crush on—yet he had brown hair and, supposedly, saw a picture of me and thought I was cute.

So I would do what any girl going through puberty with hormones coursing through her body would do: I got excited about this possibility. They dragged out this charade for a month or more.

One day at school, I asked that friend if she had finally spoken with him when she was attending a class in this neighboring town. We were sitting together outside at lunch on the playground with a group of girls around—that was the moment they thought it best to strike and get a hit of empowerment from shitting on someone else.

That someone today was me.

They looked at each other and died laughing, then began to say I was an idiot, and they made him up to see what I would do. He wasn't even a REAL person.

I was mortified and so damn confused. Again, why the heck would anybody even have the notion or idea to do something so ridiculous and hateful? Waiting for the right moment for me to get my hopes up, be invested, and then act like I was an idiot in front of everyone.

This was humiliating.

Yet my journey with that friend wouldn't end until our senior year in high school, when I was gratefully released from her grip. It culminated in a twisted story that made me the villain to yet another friend.

I will admit I played my part, and I genuinely believe accountability is essential in every situation—it takes two to tango in every relationship. But at this point, I didn't even fight for the truth. I was so drained of all the shenanigans over the years that I said eff it and let the other friendship go. I didn't fight for her, and she didn't ask to hear my side of the story either.

I let the "convenience friend" burn it all down so that she could look like a good person. I was so stuck, so insecure, and didn't have it in me to explain my perspective and gain approval.

Looking back, it was meant to be.

Where the Approval-Seeking Began

Flashing back to that younger version of me—when I was in elementary school— my mother was going through a tumultuous season. She was grappling with her own reality of my grandmother's passing and the enormous workload placed upon her. She did the best she could do.

I am sure her nervous system was shot. She was exhausted from burning the midnight oil—both required and driven by her co-dependent nature. When she was able to be present with us—mainly on weekends and some later evenings—she was fun, connected, and so creative.

I genuinely believe she had so much riding on her—her own personal integrity—that it began to create people-pleasing habits in me. When we had the opportunity to do things together, those encounters would sometimes end with her letting me know how I could have improved my "performance" for those around me. She didn't actually call it "performance." Still, over time, that is what it was. It taught me that I was wrong when I spoke up or pushed a boundary toward someone else.

She was on the edge, not living in her feminine, nurturing self. She was in her full masculine—get the job done, forward motion, achieve it now, to-do-list galore, do-it-right energy. She was a powerhouse.

When those friends were making fun of me, I had nothing to stand on. My legs were wobbly, my voice was shaky, and I didn't have the confidence to say FU when my "friend" was being an asshole. I was dripping in people-pleasing, smooth-it-over, make-sure-the-other-person-is-ok energy.

The "convenience friend" was now part of the group of friends I had created—the girls I had met and loved. The other girls and I giggled with delight and had the most insanely fun times. Somehow, in late middle school, she ended up in it as well, so I would continue to be the bullseye from time to time when it was my turn.

All of this to say, I was NEVER meant to be friends with her for as long as I was. It was a friendship of convenience, insecurities, and bad habits.

I learned so many lessons about what I do not want in a friendship—and can now spot it a mile away.

The Lesson

The approval seeker showed up many times in this friendship, and here's what I learned:

People will show you who they are—don't sugarcoat shit that happens to you repeatedly.

Find the divine lesson within the friendship and learn to let them move along their way. It's okay to leave those friendships—even if you have a lot of history—if you have spoken to that friend and they never learn. Leave, my love.

The Boomerang Effect

Be watchful of what I call the boomerang effect: when the Divine needs you to learn a lesson with a particular type of personality. Perhaps you cut a friend out of your life who never respects you, and soon you meet a new friend. After some time together, you notice they have similar tendencies to the previous friend.

This is a clue that you are the one who needs to grow and expand.

It doesn't mean they need to stay around. However, if you keep attracting it, you need to start questioning: What in YOU matches that energy? What is the story you keep telling yourself that they keep showing up in your life? Once you heal it, that personality will leave or no longer bother you—either way is a win.

Reflection Questions

Take a moment to look at your own friendships—past and present. Be honest with yourself:

1. **Is there someone from your past that you can relate to this story?** Someone who repeatedly showed you who they were, but you kept giving them chances?

2. **Are you allowing yourself to stay in a friendship right now that you know is not suitable for you?** One that hurts you or that you've outgrown? My badass lady, it's okay to let it go.

3. **What pattern keeps showing up in your friendships?** If you keep attracting the same type of person, what does that tell you about what you need to heal or learn?

Remember: Some friends are here for life, and some are intended to teach you a lesson and catapult you into the person you are meant to be and the new friendship you are calling forward.

CHAPTER 5
GUIDANCE FROM THE DIVINE

The first time I consciously sensed the guidance of God, Source, and Angels was during my elementary years. As previously stated in prior chapters, I had lost a grandma, and I now felt disconnected from the only other safe female who was consistent in my life, my mom. I remember feeling numb, lost, stepping through the motions and days that came next. During these years, I am sure that I have been assisted by divine guidance many times, as I believe we all are.

The Day I Got Lost

One fall day, we were out as a family cutting wood on a ranch my grandfather, mother, and her brothers had bought. It is a gorgeous piece of land nestled between two mountain ranges, with a river flowing along the outer edge of the property. Open hay fields are greeted by large old cottonwood trees dancing in the breeze.

It was a fun place to run, explore, and take turns chasing my cousins when they were there, playing make-believe games. On this crisp day, my parents were cutting down trees—not only to clear paths that needed opening but also to take the wood home and use it to heat our home for winter.

The gravel pit bordered the ranch, divided only by the river that separated the two properties. The summer had melted all the snow and sent the water down the river to irrigate people's grass and produce hay for the animals in and around neighboring states. The river was lower right now, and there were places you could cross easily on the culverts to get to the gravel pit from the ranch.

I still don't know what inspired the idea to go to the gravel pit when they were done cutting wood for the day, but instead of driving all the way around, they decided to walk through the trees across the field and cross the river where it was low.

I was bouncing along behind my family, slowly lagging farther and farther behind. I kept tripping over my shoelace, so I stopped in the tall grass and decided to tie it—without telling anyone.

The Shoe-Tying That Changed Everything

We were halfway to the gravel pit, and I had been practicing tying my shoes. I was so excited to see if I could do it this time and tell Mom and Dad.

I did the thing—made the bunny ear, took the left string, and wrapped it around the ear. Then I had to pause and try to repeat what I had been taught. Aha, through the hole it went. I tightened it, adjusted it, and was thrilled! I couldn't believe it! I did it!

I popped out of the grass to yell, "Mom, Dad, look what I did!" as the words started to push past my throat. All I got was a "mmmm."

I looked left, right, and in front of me. I turned swiftly to look behind me.

Nothing.

They weren't there—none of them. Like a figment of my imagination—they had disappeared. I was so confused. Where had they gone? How long had I been tying my shoe?

Surely they were right ahead of me, so I started walking toward the river—no one, not a soul in sight. I began to feel my heart race and the tears well up in my eyes. A dark feeling set over me as I whirled around, looking at the trees, open fields, and the river next to me.

I was alone. I was lost. I was afraid.

I didn't know what to do or how to cross a river on my own. I was still perplexed about how I got so far behind. As I started crying and hollering "Mom, Dad" repeatedly, I felt a calmness—a deep sense of peace—come over me, and a voice that wasn't mine but was soothing, calm, and firm that said, "Go to the truck."

I could barely see the truck. It was off in the distance, where we had crossed the property, but I listened. It was a deep, comforting voice that felt safe.

I genuinely believe, to this day, that was the voice of the Divine guiding a lost child to safety.

I went to the truck, knowing they would eventually have to come back. Now, as a kid, time felt like it moved so slowly, like a snail—twenty minutes felt like two hours. I somehow opened the door to this truck and sat up in its single cab, looking out at the trees.

I felt so alone and creeped out. I didn't like being alone, even in daylight.

I sat there for what felt like eternity. It was probably three minutes in real life, but for a child, it felt like an hour.

I should've stayed there and listened to that voice. But remember me—hi, I am Rachel. I do the things that pop into my brain, even if they come with a dash of fear.

I got out of the truck and decided to walk up the other side of the long pasture to the road—an old, paved country road. Surely someone there would know where my parents were.

So I did. I trekked through the pasture and up the slope to finally make it to the busier road. I stood there for a moment, and soon I heard bicyclists. They were surprised as they came around the corner. They slowed down as I said, "Have you seen my parents?"

Their eyes widened as they said, "No, sorry, we haven't," yet they kept going.

Yes. I said that: a lost child on a random country road, with no one in sight, and they chose to keep pedaling. Who does that?

So I started walking in the direction I believed led to the gravel pit's entrance. Mind you, this would be a half-mile walk, but I was clueless. I was shuffling along with tears rolling down my face when a truck pulled up next to me.

He rolled down the window and asked if I was okay.

"No, I am lost, and I don't know where my parents are. We were supposed to go to the gravel pit," I said.

"What are your parents' names?" he asked, so I told him.

He replied, "Oh, I know them. Hop in, would you like me to take you to them?"

Now the tears were pouring out of my face. I held it together decently in order not to panic, but when other humans were holding me with compassion, all the floodgates opened, and the sorrow poured out.

"Yes," I said as I was climbing into his truck.

I didn't know this person. I was a child. Times were different back in the eighties, and although that could've been a horrid situation, I truly believe God and divine guidance were shifting cards rapidly to help get this lost child into the hands of her parents.

He was a good guy, and thankfully, he did know my parents. He swiftly drove to the gravel pit and arrived to find my mom in the large machinery, ready to break down the front gates because no one had keys. Running to try and find me wasn't going to be fast enough once she finally realized I wasn't there.

This God-given angel in disguise slammed his truck into park and jumped out, waving his arms at my mom, who was barreling toward the gate in a 966 Cat Loader. He started yelling, "I have her! I have her!"

My mom didn't know what he was saying, so she skidded to a stop right before the gate and scampered out of the loader, her eyes bugging out as she saw me clumsily getting out of the passenger side of his truck.

I ran to her, and she picked me up, tears in her eyes, and hugged me tightly. She still refers to that gentleman as her "angel in disguise."

The Angel on the Stairs

At some point in those same years, I was at elementary school, walking down the steps of that two-story building. I had been feeling lonely and had been in what I referenced as a feeling of being "numb."

As I took a step down the stairs, I looked up at a statue of a bronze horse hanging half off the wall, midway down the steps.

I paused.

Right before my own eyes, hovering by the statue, was what I believe to have been an angel. She immediately warmed and slowed my soul with peace and love, and a knowing that I was going to be okay and that I was deeply supported, vastly loved, and profoundly cared for.

No one else seemed to notice her.

It was a brief few seconds, but I will never forget what I saw—and I will keep the rest to myself, holding her communication deeply in my heart.

I told my mom of my encounter that day, along with telling her I felt numb inside when she asked if I was okay. I am sure she thought I was seeing things, but it was enough to make her realize I needed more. I needed to spend more time with her and feel more connected.

She then began the tradition of pulling me out of school once a year to create a "ditch day"—a day she would take me to a larger neighboring town for a girls' shopping and connection day.

I noticed a shift that brought her out of the deep grief and into the next stage—a stage in which I would feel her presence more. A stage in which her heart healed a little.

Things started looking better.

The Lesson

I believe we are being guided every day, every hour, every minute, every second. Every day, there are angels in disguise ready to help you out of a tricky situation.

Even though this period of my life felt so significantly lonely—especially the part of getting lost—**we are never alone.** Our guides and God are with us.

We need to seek their guidance and wisdom. Once I started connecting with them daily, I have never felt alone, even when I am by myself.

I listened to that voice and went to the truck—that was where they knew I would be safe, where my parents would most likely return quickly.

However, when I decided to change the course of my safety, they sent another angel in disguise. They rerouted his path in pure perfection of Divine timing to find a lost child walking down the street.

I try to listen to the first notion that comes to me nowadays, but I know they have had to reroute their perfect path a few times as my stubborn butt questions it or changes direction swiftly.

I am always grateful for their guidance and the safety they provided that day.

Reflection Questions

Your intuition is your direct line to the Divine. These questions will help you strengthen that connection:

1. **Do you listen to the nudging of that inner voice?** Do you recognize that your inner intuition is connected to God, Source, and your guides?

2. **What will you do differently next time your intuition red-flags you?** Will you push past it because it doesn't make sense, or will you humor it and take a calculated risk toward where you are being guided?

3. **Do you connect with your guides daily?** What type of practices could you incorporate to let them know you are available for clearer, more precise guidance?

4. **Do you feel weird about connecting with divine guidance?** Know this: They can sense your hesitation. The more transparent and consistent you are with them, the stronger your connection becomes.

CHAPTER 6
THE SILENT AGREER

The Latch-Key Years

A lot happened in elementary school: fun times, giggling with friends I was getting to know, and a lot of wild, free time at home. Learning how to help my mom clean this new house they built, which felt like a mansion compared to the trailer we had lived in before.

Summers felt like they lasted forever. A growing love of horses was humming in the depths of my heart. Memories of riding to my bestie's house down the county road—yes, this happened before sixth grade. It was a different time, that is for sure.

There was still a wild, free feeling among the kids back then, and I got to experience it regularly while riding my horse a few miles away, heading to my bestie's house for a horse sleepover. Mind you, we thought it would be a blast to set up "house" in the stock horse trailer and sleep in it outside. It got cold, but we made it happen.

We were young and willing to push the limits of what my now-adult self likes—gorgeous hotel rooms with soft, beautiful bedding—over camping in any form. True.

There was freedom back in the day, complete with long summers accompanied by daily chores to help keep the house running smoothly with two very busy working parents.

The Working Moms and Latch-Key Kids

You see, my mom was in the generation of working moms. Not only was she already known as a hard worker because of her background, but now, for the first time, women had full rights. It was almost expected that they would work to bring in a double income.

This was the latch-key kids' era. We knew how to make our own meals, clean the house, do the chores, and do our homework before our parents were home—or at least try. My parents did most of the cooking, and I remember countless days of waking up to my dad making a full, healthy breakfast before we were shoved onto a school bus with a very intense driver who made everybody mind their manners in fear of her yelling.

We knew that once school was out, we would be home alone for a few hours until my parents finished their work for the day. My dad arrived home first at about 5:30 and was able to help with evening tasks. It was a very independent time for kids whose parents worked.

What I Longed For

Although I had a wonderful childhood, I longed for that deep connection that wasn't being met by the generation of American mothers who had to work full-time and then take on full-time duties once home.

My father is one of the most patient people I know—he is kind and knowledgeable as well—but no man can comfort a girl the way a mother can. Although he tried, I needed her. He was always there, picking up any slack that my mom couldn't. He sometimes made dinner, and most of the time made breakfast. His quietness was loud for me as a talkative girl, and I didn't know what to do with the attention I was seeking.

I wanted to be wild, free, understood, seen, loved, and nurtured at times—that is what my feminine soul needed.

As a kid, I didn't know these things, but I knew something was lacking. There was an emptiness inside that needed a little more.

Occasionally, on weekends, we would get together with some of my parents' friends. One specifically had a boy the same age as my brother, who was a few years older than me.

The parents would be playing cards downstairs, and you could hear the laughter erupting every few minutes. They were good people with huge hearts. Their son was also a good person. However, he was entering puberty and had all the raging hormones any teenager could handle.

When Silence Became Survival

One night, while we were visiting, laughter flowed downstairs among the adults, and my brother, a hungry teenage boy, joined them to eat more food.

I was upstairs with his friend. This "friend" coerced me to climb up on his top bunk, he made me lie down, and then he proceeded to touch the private areas of my body.

I was so unbelievably uncomfortable with it, yet I lay there terrified. Terrified to say anything. He was bigger, older, and was supposed to be wiser than me. I felt stuck, motionless, and unable to breathe. I held my breath and froze at that moment.

He convinced me this was a good thing, that I was so pretty, and that this was normal behavior.

There have been multiple generations of women who were told not to speak of "inappropriate topics"—such as periods and sex. They genuinely had a hard time being clear with their daughters about what was appropriate touch, and also that when you reach a certain age, your period begins. It is not their fault that this was the energy around these topics. I have spoken with many friends from my generation who said their moms didn't inform them of these difficult conversations; therefore, the pattern repeats. And the next generation is clueless until it's happening.

I didn't have a voice. I was trapped.

In the early elementary grades, I didn't have the words, and the people-pleaser that was starting to develop was paralyzed by fear of disappointing anyone.

It was clear that I could be taken advantage of.

It lasted a while. I am sure he heard my brother coming back up the stairs, and he quickly jumped down off the top bunk, leaving me stunned and scared.

I thought I would be in trouble. I thought I was bad and dirty and somehow deserved to be touched in inappropriate, uncomfortable ways that I didn't permit. I convinced myself I had clearly asked for it, and I didn't want to be ashamed of telling anyone, so I didn't.

The only person who knew about this was my husband, until now.

I shared this book with my mother first, and when she heard it, she was horrified and cried; her heart was so hurt, as any mother would be upon hearing such news.

She proclaimed, "You could've come to me", but if you have been in this situation, it doesn't always feel that way; instead, you take the shame to your own heart instead of seeing it as a violation upon yourself.

The Lesson

This is where the "silent agreer" came into play—and I need you to hear this:

It wasn't me. I wasn't nasty, dirty, or had even given the inclination that this was what I wanted.

I was scared and couldn't scream for fear I would get in trouble and be deemed "bad" in some way. I had stepped into the early stages of my people-pleasing journey, and this wasn't the first time I would be used because I cared more about pleasing others than taking care of myself.

For Anyone Carrying Violations

When you are a people pleaser, you can't stand up for yourself against the ways you are being violated. But hear me:

There is nothing wrong with you or dirty about you.

You were violated by someone who was older or knew better. YOU should not carry the shame. Find a way to let it out of your body—it is not yours to hold, my love.

Seek counseling or EMDR in more severe cases. Release what was never yours to carry.

Reflection Questions

These questions may bring up difficult emotions. Take your time. Find a safe space. Be gentle with yourself.

1. **Where in your life right now are you bowing down to something or someone that is hurting you?** Where are you saying it's okay, but your body is churning with hurt, pain, disgust, discomfort, and anger? It's not OK. I am permitting you to stand up for yourself and say NO—not just NO, but FUCK NO.

2. **Where are you carrying someone else's shame for what they did to you?** If you need to speak to a counselor—to say it out loud to someone who can't tell anyone—then do it. Release it. It is not yours to hold.

3. **Are you giving your body in your intimate relationship without truly wanting to?** Have you felt most of your life as though you need to "give" your body to please someone else, yet you don't understand true pleasure? Are you participating in the act, whether you really want to or not?

Untamed Bonus: A Note on Sexual Reclaiming

There is a collective conditioning about what sex should be; it may have been your first experiences with sex, or perhaps something you were told or shown.

If you were violated in any way, there might now be dis-regulated energy in your body, making it unclear whether you can say "No". No to any form of being touched.

I am permitting you to say, "Wait, I need a minute." To say "No." To even state to your husband or spouse that you are giving without fully feeling open and willing inside your body—and that is making you feel really uncomfortable.

This can be traumatic to the feminine. It's okay to find other ways to connect for a bit while you reconnect with your pleasure. Find it within yourself. Find it by speaking up and guiding your partner to what actually feels good. Connect with them through hours of foreplay that doesn't actually lead to penetration.

The goal is to be very clear if it is okay to take it all the way, or if you need to rebuild and release so you can come fully into that sexual goddess that is layered underneath all the shame or "have-to's you have been taught as a woman."

Believe me, if you actively work toward knowing how to really turn yourself on, how to allow your body to give permission instead of being forced—your spouse will love it because you will be so much more connected when you engage in intimacy with that person.

CHAPTER 7
THE PEACEMAKER

Middle School and New Beginnings

Moving on to middle school, my mom had shifted her schedule and was able to be home with us a little more. She was healing and finding a new rhythm in her work-life balance, as it had been a few years since my grandma had passed. She had become a pro at bookkeeping, was running a couple of companies, and had hired an office man to help her handle accounts receivable. Although she was still heavily committed to her work, there was a better flow of energy in our home.

Middle school is a hard time for most kids. The raging hormones, body changes, and changes in schools and schedules are giant leaps into the unknown. Everyone feels awkward yet suddenly interested in the opposite sex in a way they thought was once disgusting and repulsive. It truly is a weird dimension to step into.

The shifting hormones and the true beginning of team sports make it an excellent opportunity for a new layer of competitive spirit to arise among middle school kids.

The Rules and the Lessons

All those years of riding my horse down the county road with my mom at work had her worried each time I did it. My parents made a rule: if I wanted to ride over to my friends, I had to call my mom the moment I arrived from the landline—no, we didn't have cell phones "back then"—and if I didn't call within about fifteen minutes of when I should've arrived, the phone would be ringing at my friend's house. I was told to get back on my horse; the playdate was over, and I had to ride my butt back home because I was now grounded.

As a kid, I was so irritated. I had barely begun playing with my friend, and I knew I was fine. As an adult, I understand and think "rightfully so" that I got grounded, as I can't imagine my daughter riding down the county road by herself on her horse at that age and then not letting me know she was safe.

My mom had a few too many nervous moments and decided to find riding lessons for me. She grew up in high school rodeo; it's among her best childhood memories. She was an excellent barrel racer, but her real love was for running poles on her horse Scarlett. She knew the love of a little girl and her horse—it was unstoppable and untamed—and she didn't want to deter that. However, she needed me to have more knowledge and safety around handling a horse, so off to lessons she sent me.

I disliked playing team sports. I joined middle school basketball in sixth and seventh grade, but I hated it. I hated most team sports—I found them boring and a waste of my time, and I didn't feel very skilled at them because I never put my heart into them.

My heart belonged to horses. I ate, slept, and breathed horses.

I started taking lessons with a lady in a neighboring town. She was good and very safety-conscious—maybe a little too much. If the horse got a little frisky, we got off and lunged more, rather than learning the skills to ride out the bad behavior and correct it while in the saddle. However, she taught me excellent showing skills, poise, and many safety skills that still course through me as a rider today.

Finding Merle: My First Love

I needed to find a horse with a sound mind for the lessons. We had tried a few out, and she was displeased with what she had seen. I don't blame her—I had one that I named "Milky Way" (yeah, that was a weird name thinking back). He was a flea-bitten grey, and he loved to rear anytime he didn't like what I was asking him to do.

For me, it was fun riding home on the county road in the rain with my mom following me in the car, making sure I was safe. He reared a few times, and she decided yes, maybe it was time to find a horse with a more willing brain. Now, as an adult, I know the ways we could've worked with him to break those habits. However, if the trainer hadn't been adamant about getting rid of him, I would have never found the first LOVE of my life in the next horse, Merle.

He was a broken-down, neglected 14.5-hand sorrel quarter horse that had done a bit of everything in his life. My parents actually bought him for my brother, who wanted to do trail riding with his friends. However, my brother's main love was sports, specifically wrestling.

We brought Merle home. He was severely underweight and looked 10 years older than he actually was. We started putting weight on him slowly, with a mixture of grains, minerals, and all the roughage he desired. After I had been through a couple of horses that this trainer deemed "untrainable," my mom finally told the trainer about my brother's new horse, who seemed willing, and that maybe we could try him for a short time.

I rode Merle in the arena for this trainer to witness, watching her with the side eye and trying to get to know this horse at the same time, wondering if this one would pass her approval test.

He did. She said we could try to work with him and see where it went.

Well, that was the day my brother lost his new horse. He never got another one, just rode Merle here and there and went on to do very well as a wrestler. We moved Merle into a stable where my trainer was, and we started "pouring the chili" into his nutrition, warming up his muscles that had melted away, and working with him on training for showing in Western pleasure and English jumping.

The following summer, while at a show, my parents ran into the previous owner while I was riding. By then, Merle had gained a hundred or more pounds, had muscled up in a beautiful round way that quarter horses do, and was slicked out, looking super healthy and feeling so good.

The previous owner looked at me and asked who this new horse was. My parents were confused. They said, "That's Merle," and his mouth dropped. He didn't even recognize the horse he had sold them.

Merle would live until he was thirty-five years old, and he would be a horse I would always feel connected to. He was a God-send for me in trying times, and we had a deep, trusting connection.

We took him in. We saved him, nurturing his health, and he saved my spirit in return.

The Forced Apology

As I was succeeding in some stiff competition, I had a friend who decided she wanted to take lessons from this trainer. As young friends, we thought it would be so fun. She brought in a young horse and wasn't having the same success I was at that time.

Jealousy hit hard. Situations weren't handled well, and that friendship—which was also a second-generation friendship, created by my mom and hers—fizzled. Not just fizzled, more like blew up. It was ugly and accentuated living in a small town full of gossipers.
You see, I didn't like regular sports—I loved competing on my horse. The

problem, however, is that you might be competing against your friends, which is different from team sports, when you and your friends are together competing against a rival town.

Looking back, I realized how deeply I was people-pleasing. I don't think I knew it then—I just knew my discomfort.

Some ugly things had happened in the friendship, and of course, it takes two. My part felt small compared to what they had done to me, just because I was beating their daughter in horse shows.

However, I was told that I needed to apologize to this other friend.

The Phone Call

I remember making that phone call. First, I was never fully validated in the pain they sent my way, the hurt I had felt from their actions, just because I was succeeding at something I put the time and hard work into. My friend was also working hard, but you can't expect a young child to win when you put them on a green horse that is still learning fundamental skills.

We were both working toward our goals, and there could have been a genuine gathering and a sense of caring for each family and their goals, instead of the Hatfield-McCoy breakout.

Back to the phone call: I remember calling her, still frustrated that she hadn't apologized to me for other things that had happened. I apologized to her on the phone, even though every piece of me inside wanted to blurt out how she had hurt me as well, and I didn't feel bad for the little instance I was "having" to speak of.

I remember her reaction was pure victimhood: she was the "only one hurt," "I was the worst person," and she might never be able to be my friend again.

Ick.
There was never an acknowledgment of the hurt that they caused. But my

mom was the "bigger" person and knew how to guide me to apologize for the part I was responsible for.

They instead got stuck in the small-town mindset, and instead of taking ownership, they stood in vats of deep victimhood, letting everyone in town know how terrible we were.

There are a few circles like this. If you live in a small town, they are unavoidable, yet powerful in the wrong way.

Our friendships ended there. I stopped going to that trainer because my parents aren't the type to stay in the "popular crowd," gossiping to fit in. I continued competing and joined a drill team on horseback, which was among the best memories I had with my childhood girlfriends.

My entire life was dedicated to the next adventure on my new horse, Merle.

The Lesson

This was the Peacemaker showing up and trying to make everything alright, even when she didn't feel it herself.

Muscles and intuition don't lie. You might misread them sometimes, but if you are in tune, they will always guide you.

My entire body revolted that day—the day I had to apologize and was met with a victim mentality. It is essential to know you are valid in these situations. If you have feelings around a problem, you need to listen to them and let them be heard. You need to know that it is also safe for you to have feelings in a challenging situation.

As adults, we can't just fly off the handle every time our feelings get hurt, but learning to acknowledge and validate our feelings ourselves is a skill worth having.

When Apologies Matter (And When They Don't)

Not every situation needs an apology, especially if it is forced. If you have genuinely done something wrong, when you recognize it in your heart, send a sincere apology. Don't just apologize because of your people-pleasing fear of not being liked.

The real gold that gets discovered along the way? Apologizing to yourself for those situations and offering yourself grace.

Reflection Questions

"The Sorry" is one of the most common—and most damaging—people-pleasing patterns. It's time to break it.

1. **Where in your life are you over-apologizing?** Think about today, this week. How many times did you say "I'm sorry" for things that weren't your fault? For basic human needs like eating, using the bathroom, or taking up space?

2. **What is one thing you can do differently today to stop showing up as a "sorry human being?"** Choose one situation in which you typically apologize, and practice staying silent or saying something neutral instead.

3. **Are you watering down the power of "sorry?"** Don't be the person "crying sorry" like the boy who cried wolf. Each time you say "sorry" for something that wasn't an actual wrongdoing, you dilute a powerful word for when it's really necessary. Where can you reclaim the weight of a genuine apology?

Untamed Bonus: A Challenge

This week, catch yourself every time you start to say "I'm sorry." Pause. Ask yourself: "Did I actually do something wrong, or am I just existing?"

Stop apologizing for basic human needs. Stop apologizing for taking up space. Stop apologizing for having feelings, needs, or opinions.

You are allowed to exist without a constant apology.

CHAPTER 8
FOMO

High School and Hard Lessons

Oh, high school—I have so many incredible friendship memories from all the horse adventures, giggles, and fun times. However, this book wasn't titled "All the Best Times in My Life." It was written with the intention of sharing the hard times, vulnerabilities, and mistakes in my life, with lessons and takeaways to help you relate and rise into a better version of yourself.

So I will continue with the mistakes and hard things in my life, hoping that it helps you ascend with a fierce knowing and rebirth into who you are meant to be. And that, my love, is not a people pleaser or follower.

Speaking of being a follower—yeah, it happened to me. Of course it did. We're going to go there.

In many areas of my life, I knew what I wanted, especially when it came to my horse. However, by the time I went to high school, I had learned some hard lessons in humility from being made fun of and from losing friendships I cared about because somehow I didn't nurture them enough.

I was getting good at making others feel better than I cared about how I felt, because to make others feel good was a people pleaser's number one job—and I was on my way to being employee of the month.

My Original Girl Bestie

I loved my OG bestie, the one I always got in trouble with because we literally had too much fun and forgot to clue my parents in. She is still my OGB, and we will always have a friendship that no one will divide. We respect each other and the other friendships in each other's lives, and we encourage each other in the good and hard times of our adult lives.

There weren't always good times. We have gone through a few times when we had to take a few years apart, yet somehow, we both calibrate and find each other rising to the next level. We are meant to rise together, not slow each other down or drag each other along.

That is what deeply connected feminine friendships, and sisterhood do: they allow space, dive into the deep, and invite—not drag.

The New Friend Who Hurt My OGB

I met a new friend in late middle school who remained a friend in high school. She lived down the lane from my OGB, and we fell into our friendship hard—one of those kindred-spirit connections. She ended up joining the drill team I was on as one of the original members who started the group in our small town, and we spent a ton of time together.

She had a distaste for my OGB and did small things to hurt her.

I wanted everyone to be happy—I am an eternal optimist, so I see the good in most everyone—and that piece of me had the ostrich sticking its head in the sand trait. I didn't know until years later that this new friend used to call my bestie and tell her that, on the days I was coming over, I got to spend time with this new friend—not her.

I still rode my horse or walked down the county road—that was my mode of transportation in the summers when my chores were done, and my parents were at work. I never called my OGB and bragged that I would be passing by her house on my way to another friend's house. I would be quiet, walking by, hoping her cute little dog, Copper, wasn't outside barking at me so that I wouldn't hurt her feelings.

One day, I arrived at my new friend's house, and she dialed my bestie to let her know that she and I were having a great time together and that my OGB wasn't invited.

Call me dumb, but I sat there mortified that it came so naturally to hurt someone like that. I did speak up on the phone that day and say something I can't remember, but I do know it deeply hurt that friend to realize it was true, and we were rubbing it in her face.

That was the first time I realized I was acting like a follower and didn't speak up.

The Classroom Walkout

Another pivotal time was more public. I was a freshman or sophomore—to be honest, I don't remember useless details—so hang in there with me, ha ha.

By now, I had two new friends who were on the drill team together, living our best life. Then the "convenience" friend must've felt left out, so she joined the drill team as well. We now had a group of us that went to school, took classes together, and rode every week. We were submerged.

Three of us were in a history class together that semester. One day, our teacher was in the middle of a lesson, and my two closest friends in the class started debating what he was saying. I was thinking, "Yeah, what they said"—even though I had no business sticking my nose in their battle against the teacher.

I was wearing my "follower" outfit that day and felt compelled to do what my friends were doing.

After a few sentences were thrown back and forth, and the teacher seemed to be getting angrier, I watched my friends get up and storm out of the class. The next part sucks to admit, but I didn't want to feel dumb, like I didn't know what the hell they were speaking of or doing. So what did I do?

Yep—I got up, said something dumb like "Yeah, I agree with them," and marched my little butt out into the hallway following them.

When the door shut behind me and my eyes met theirs, their laughter turned into wide-eyed shock.

"Rachel, what are you doing?" they questioned.

"I agree with you guys," I said.

Right as I finished the sentence, the door shut behind me, with the teacher right in front of me as I turned around. I waited to hear how we were to march to the principal's office and what we were to get in trouble for.

Instead, I was met with laughter and the teacher saying, "That was awesome"—mainly to my friends—and then he looked at me, laughing, and said, "What was that all about? I wasn't expecting you to march out."

Oh, my embarrassment was for sure seen that day as red covered my entire body. They had staged a ruse that I decided to butt my little, insecure head into to make sure I wasn't left out of my circle.

Shit. I had just been exposed to the piece of my heart that had a flare of wanting to fit in. My heart felt like it was outside my body, as if everyone were seeing and judging me.

It became a classroom joke, and I had to wear the shame for the rest of the semester. Many times, I asked myself what was happening, why I would do such an embarrassing thing, and why I would feel the need to follow them into a battle that I didn't even understand.

This was a great learning lesson. I pivoted from there, but it would take a few years before I fully got rid of teenage FOMO.

Adult FOMO: The Never-Enough Trap

If you are not careful, this will follow you into adulthood. You may see what your friends or family members are doing or buying, and get trapped in this endless cycle of never having or being enough.

It is an illusion.

You are enough. You have enough. Even when they want to flaunt it in your face, ask yourself, "Would I really even want that thing?"

I decorate my home by intuition and visions of what I see there. I have always chosen the color scheme and metals that I desire, not what is on trend. Trends fade and change, making you feel like there is a never-ending cycle of not having the right décor in your home. They change so much that if you hold onto them long enough, they will come back into style, like mullets and bell-bottoms.

Do what your heart is calling you to—not because it's a trend or you need to be loved.

I didn't want to be left out of my circle, but if I had listened to my intuition, I would have recognized that I would be set free if I were.

The Lesson

The approval seeker was coursing through me and showing up as a follower that day.

On Absorbing Others' Energy

I have since learned that I can easily absorb other people's energy. I feel it so deeply and so intensely, as if it were my own feelings. That day was a combination of social pressures to fit in, be cool, be innovative, and be accepted, along with a genuine sense of the emotions they expressed in their acting. I felt the hostility toward the teacher, their rebellion, and their passion in my own body that day.

I now ask myself in moments when unexpected emotions come over me like a tidal wave: "Is this mine? What just happened?"

Most of the time, it isn't mine.

Where I Am Now

I have since learned I am okay alone. I will say no to group friend gatherings if I feel like staying home and taking a bubble bath. I don't give a shit about being left out or having FOMO because I know who I am and that I am all I need.

Reflection Questions

FOMO is a sneaky little bitch. It makes you say yes when everything in you wants to say no. It makes you spend money you don't have on things you don't even like. Take a moment to get honest about where FOMO is running your life:

1. **Who are you, really?** Not who you pretend to be for others, not who shows up to fit in—but who are you when no one is watching? What do you actually enjoy?

2. **Where are you acting out of FOMO right now?** Are you putting yourself in situations you really don't want to be in or that are uncomfortable, just because you don't want to miss out or be left out?

3. **Are you overspending to keep up appearances?** Are you buying things as an adult just to look a certain way? Or are you buying a bunch of cheap stuff instead of waiting for a few beautiful, quality pieces you actually love?

4. **Do you get caught up in what others have?** Do you think it will make you happy, without actually considering whether it is really your style or desire? What would change if you bought only what truly lights you up?

A Truth to Remember

You are enough as you are. You don't need to keep up with anyone. The only person you need to impress is the one looking back at you in the mirror.

CHAPTER 9
WASTED TIME

High school was better than the emotional and hormonal rollercoaster of middle school. I had a good group of friends, I was in full-time horse activities after school, and, of course, had gone on a couple of dates with boys. Life was good; I knew how to nurture others to the extreme people-pleasing level and worry endlessly if I messed up in any way… what could go wrong?

At the beginning of my sophomore year, I was allowed to go on dates with boys, but I didn't want anything serious. I would go on a few dates but never let any one guy commit as an actual long-term boyfriend. I was more interested in horse activities, which kept me busy. At this time, I could drive, and in my spare time on weekends, I was a hostess at a local café. It was fun, and I had to get up early because they opened at 6 a.m. One morning, this guy came in. I sat him and his friend at a table, left them with their menus, and went back to my hostess post. I caught him looking at me a few times out of the corner of my eye. It was noticeable he had something he wanted to say to me. I went on about my job, and when they were done eating, they brought their ticket to me to check out at the register. He was taller than me, with a baseball player's build and blue eyes. He asked me to go on a date with him and made it nearly impossible for me to say no. So I accepted and gave him my phone number.

On our first date, he told me it wasn't the first time he had asked me out. What? I was confused. However, apparently, about six months prior, we had been at a local teenager hangout, and he had approached me. It was dark outside, so I didn't remember him as clearly. At that time, I had been on a few dates with another guy, so when Zack approached, I, of course, wasn't interested in dating two guys at once, so I blew him off—nicely, but with confidence. Well, apparently, for him, that wasn't going to work—challenge accepted. He didn't know who I was, but running into me at that café inspired him to try again and not take no for an answer. He told me later that his friend had teased him for being so brazen when they left the restaurant. There was something about him that drew me in, something different about him; he had a slight tinge of that bad-boy thing going on, and I had never dated anyone like him.

We went on a couple of dates over the next few weeks, and things naturally turned more serious. I met his mom within the first two weeks of dating him. She had been diagnosed with cancer and was sadly losing that battle. It was tragic—something I hadn't experienced before. I had experienced the deaths and funerals of elderly family members and a friend's mom, whom I hadn't known very well. This was different. I was starting to like this guy, and he had something challenging to face in the months ahead. She passed away within a couple of months of my calling him my boyfriend, and that heart-wrenching experience connected us in a bond more profound than I had ever experienced at that point. Remember me—I am an open center, people-pleaser wanting to pour out everything from my heart. So, of course, what did I do? I started pouring into him and his dad, bringing them meals and cookies every single week. We started hanging out constantly. He wasn't like anyone I had met; he snagged me good. He was smooth-talking and knew exactly how to reel me in when I wasn't seeming super interested in the relationship any longer. It was as though he knew how to play on all my insecurities, and new ones were popping up weekly.

Six months had passed, and a friend called to tell me he had cheated on me with another local girl I knew. I was shocked and didn't believe her. Let's just say the girl he supposedly cheated on me with was not the best source of truth. I had a talk with him, and he so smoothly denied, denied, denied, and reassured. I had no idea, but this guy was so damn good at manipulation. This went on and off over the next few years.

Do you ever ask yourself why you would stay in a relationship for so long when you knew better? Well, that's the thing—typically, you can't see it clearly; hindsight is 20/20. He was good. Good at manipulating and getting his way, good at talking me out of any ideas, good at covering his ass, and so freaking good at smoothing things over! He was a master at these techniques. I was a people-pleaser with pure optimism pulsing through my veins, so although my freaking intuition kept saying "something is off," he smoothed it out like creamy peanut butter on crunchy toast every single time. I was a fool. Later, I realized that every time he cheated, he would bring me flowers—big, gorgeous flowers. It was sickening. I believed him. I believed he was right, and I believed I had just become a jealous type, that it was my insecurity and shortcomings. My self-confidence—the one that was high before meeting him—was blown. I didn't have anything left after playing these games repeatedly.

I questioned myself even more. I didn't have a leg to stand on. My friendships were dwindling at the end of high school due to other drama. I had spent so much time with him instead of them, had been through some major emotional times with him, and I thought I "loved" him. Was love supposed to be this hard? This wavering? Was it supposed to be this good, then this bad? This questioning? This doubting?

I remember having a random conversation with a gentleman who had been divorced, and I remember asking him if there were signs before he married the woman he would go on to have a harrowing separation with. He said, "Yes, there was a gut feeling it wasn't right." Oh boy, could he be right? Was this what I was feeling? This "gut" feeling? Remember that confidence thing? Yeah, it was obliterated. So guess what—I didn't think I could find a better guy, I didn't know I could have a better relationship. Yep, I thought, "Well, this is it. This is the best I can do." Things were good, things were bad; this is just normal in relationships.

I had fallen for him because he needed me; he needed my empathy and caring nature to get through his mom's passing. I should have moved on shortly after her passing. We were not meant to be together, but I stayed with him because my brain was now warped with ideas and mental games. I was miserable but couldn't imagine being without him. That sucks. Who the fuck was I? This was a new version of me I had never met, and I didn't like her. There were times I was afraid of him. Once, I asked my mom to pick me up from his house because it nearly turned physical. I was shaken and didn't want him to drive me home. But mainly, it was his mental and emotional games that were so freaking smooth and, over time, hollowed out my soul. My mom said she and my father got to the point they were scared—scared that if she and my dad made any quick movements or demands, I would bolt with him. Yet that never even crossed my mind. I wasn't about to run away with the guy; I just couldn't wrap my head around how to get out of a relationship with him. I loved my home, my family, and my horse. My parents had seen my self-esteem tank, and I don't want to know what that would be like as a parent. He was a huge lesson in my life, and I would spend years afterward in confusion about why it took me so damn long to break up with him.

A year and a half before I broke up with him, a trainer I was working out with asked me if he was the one I wanted to marry. I jokingly scoffed and said, "No." She started laughing, and I thought, "Yeah, that is weird—why would I be with a guy for three years now if I knew, deep down, I didn't want a future commitment with him?" I knew deep down it needed to end, but each time I would try, he would work his manipulative magic and reel me back in, like a fish about to die on the end of a line. I broke up with him after four and a half years of dating. At that time, I was out of high school and attending cosmetology school. I genuinely believe I went to cosmetology school simply for God to put me in a different environment and help me build my confidence so I could see how much I didn't like where this relationship was headed. Toward the end of my time as a cosmetology student, I finally had the nerve to say no over and over again as he pleaded with me to stay. The tables had turned. My spine had started erecting again, and the door creaked open into the room where my confidence lived. I had a sliver, and I wasn't turning back.

There were many lessons during my relationship with Zack. Even though it was on a rocket ship to disaster land, a nugget of what I did want was shown to me. Zack and I had been at an auto body shop getting something for his truck. We were sitting in the waiting room while another gentleman was checking out at the counter. You couldn't help overhearing the conversation between this gentleman and the clerk. The man was lit up with love and joy as he spoke about his wife, who wasn't there. He talked about all the right things: how she was the love of his life, that he didn't care where they lived, what she wore, or what she drove, that he was over the moon with this woman, and that they had been married for seventeen years. I had never in my pea-picking life heard a manly man, let alone any man, talk about his wife in that manner. Zack seemed not to be in the same room or hearing this conversation; he was focused on when this employee would finish with this other guy and be able to serve him. As I listened to this gentleman ooze his love and passion for his wife, rockets of desire shot from my heart. If I had been a cartoon, hearts would have appeared in my eyes with pure desire. I wanted a man who loved me so deeply, so passionately, and so outwardly! I wanted that kind of love—real and safe—like a distant memory I hoped could come true. Little did I know those rocket ships of desire were being planted for my future.

The Lesson

I learned so much from this relationship—hard, painful lessons I needed to face. I learned not to sacrifice my happiness, my hobbies, my time, and my friendships for a relationship that, deep down, felt questionable. I realized that it's never too late to get out.

Suppose you have an inkling that pings you often, hinting that the relationship is not meant to be yours, listen to it. Your intuition is trying to give you information. It will grow dimmer and dimmer the less you listen to it, but once you start connecting again, it will happily rebuild its relationship of trust with you.

Sadly, this ex-boyfriend went on to really mess up his life with drugs and alcohol, eventually passing away before he even turned forty. It still baffles me. But his story doesn't have to be your story. You can choose differently.

Reflection Questions

Take some time to sit with these questions. Journal your responses. Be honest, raw, and kind with yourself.

1. **Where in your life are you not listening to your intuition?** Are you in an abusive relationship, my love, and have convinced yourself no one will want you? This is the furthest thing from the truth. Even if you need to be single for a while, could you imagine the freedom that would come from doing whatever you want?

2. **Find that girl inside you.** She is in there. She isn't gone. Remember a time when you did something so brave—close your eyes and feel what it felt like. Channel that version of you. Ask her if she would stay in this relationship, and I guarantee it's a no. What does she tell you?

3. **If you do break up with them, how will you hold the pose?** It might be hard. You might feel a strong, dysfunctional pull toward that person. Call in your confidence, girl, and feel her energy in each part of your body. Say the reasons you are done out loud. Write them down.

4. **Are you a match for what you desire?** Are you a match for the guy or gal you want to be with? If not, what power moves can you start making in that direction? How does she dress, how she treats herself and others around her, and how does she spend her money and time?

5. **Already Married?** Don't just throw in the towel, even if you don't like the person anymore, counseling can truly turn it around. Give it a shot before flushing the marriage down the drain; however, if it is abusive, flush girl flush.

Remember: It will get better. There is a better match. It will happen—you have to believe. The first step is to stop wasting time waiting on what wasn't meant to be yours.

CHAPTER 10
THE FRIEND SPECTRUM

We took a step forward in the last chapter. However, I need to take one step back to tell this next story.

Senior Year: When Everything Started to Tank

I was a senior in high school, and our circle of friends from the past five years was starting to tank. Two of the five girls had graduated years prior, and three of us were left to graduate that year.

It was a challenging year.

I basically got exiled from the threesome group due to poor communication on my part. I didn't care about the "convenience friend," but I do regret not fighting harder for the other friend who was involved. We had a genuine friendship and a deep connection.

However, I was a shell of myself. I wasn't the same person. I had been with Zack for two years now, and he had done a number on my self-esteem. My friends thought he was weird—however, I couldn't see it. On the flip side, he was cute and convincing. I was stuck, but I didn't know it.

If you ever talk about another friend and find yourself asking, "Why does she stay with that person?"—most likely, she can't see how bad it is, or she thinks she is worthless and can't get out.

It was a sad year, heavy with lonely feelings at school. The saving grace was that I only had half a day of classes, so I was able to go home at lunch and move on to other things, rather than dwell on the fact that I had lost two friendships.

I didn't have it in me to fight. I was tired of the bully moves, and it felt better to let the other one go rather than argue with the "convenience friend" who loved to move in on my close friendships for her own benefit.

The Boy Who Would Change Everything

Amid all this drama and the need to focus on finishing my senior year, I didn't know what I wanted to do after high school. I come from a long line of entrepreneurs who hadn't been to college and had done well for themselves, so college was strongly encouraged but not pushed; as a result, while everyone already knew which college they would attend, I still didn't have a plan.

I was floundering in many areas of my life during my senior year. However, one thing that brought me joy was having a class with a guy I had known since second grade.

His parents had moved him from a neighboring town to our school in second grade, and he was so shy. He played basketball and would occasionally say random things to me. I always thought it was funny in elementary and middle school that he would be the first one in the lunch line, eat like a Labrador that hadn't been fed in a week, and run outside to get as much time on the court as possible during recess.

You could always find him with a basketball in hand and a "please don't talk to me" look on his face.

The Playground Wedding

In elementary school, there was a gazebo on the playground. Many girls would go out to the gazebo and instantly become inspired by their future wedding dreams.

Somehow, a couple of my friends and I convinced (although I don't think we tried very hard) three farm boys in our class that we should get married. So we each chose the guy we would marry, and it became a thing.

We had a brief conversation about which day we would hold our ceremony and that the boys should bring a ring—you know, the type you used to be able to find in the gumball machines.

The day was upon us. It would be a triple wedding in the field beyond the playground down by the cattails. The other boys were ready, but I had to get my soon-to-be husband off the basketball court.

Each couple went through and told the other their "I do's." The boys slipped on some homemade rings—probably made of twine or wire—and then they kissed—a quick peck.

It was my turn, my soon-to-be basketball husband facing me. We said our "I do's," and a quick peck on the lips sealed the deal. He pulled a ring out of his pocket like a piece of lint and handed it to me.

My eyes jumped out of their sockets—it was a real ring, a big ring. It was gold with a dark stone in the middle surrounded by diamonds, more like cubic zirconia, but I thought it was diamonds.

I put it on my ring finger, and it slid off. I tried it on my thumb, and it was too big. I told him I couldn't accept this—it's too nice—and he declined, not even allowing me to get close to him.

He quickly changed the subject and stated, "I brought a wedding cake," as he pulled out a package of graham crackers that had been shoved in his pocket. We all started grabbing one as the bell rang, signaling the end of recess and our wedding ceremonies.

We were all playground married, and we felt so mature.

That evening, my mother had to sit me down. She had received a phone call that her daughter had been witnessed kissing (a peck) a boy on the playground, and there would be no tolerance for that at this school. My mom was mortified and grounded me.

As we were talking about it, I pulled out the ring he gave me, and she said, "Rachel, you have to give that back to that boy. That looks like his mother's ring."

I told her I tried, but would try again the next day. When I approached him again, he denied that it was his mother's and wouldn't even let me continue the conversation. He went back to playing basketball, and we all moved on as if nothing had ever happened.

In middle school, he was still shy and an excellent basketball player, most likely because he ate, slept, and spent all his time playing. He lived on a farm, and if he wasn't helping his dad with all that it takes to run it, he was at school or playing basketball.

In our senior year of high school, he was just a grown-up version of that shy boy. However, he would come out of his shell a little when I sat next to him in English class. There were many opportunities in that class to have micro-minutes of chatting, and we found ourselves talking about personal topics and laughing a lot.

I really looked forward to that class because he made it so funny. He was a true ray of sunshine gleaming through on a tough year.

Graduation Day

Graduation day was upon us. He would be attending the local college, and I still hadn't decided, although I had a great job lined up as a teller at a bank in the meantime.

I graduated with those friends who basically acted as though we had never been close, and that was painful. I got good at holding in my needs and desires for the relationships around me and instead catered to what others needed more.

Although a dark cloud hung over me, I was still driven by a relentless optimism that would most likely drive some people insane. I could hold a lot—it was so deeply uncomfortable and painful—but it did not change my outer appearance to show any reflection of the storm inside. I have always been an optimist; it has been a gift and a saving grace in the more difficult times in my life.

I was grateful that the year was over and I didn't have to show up daily, put on a brave face, smile, and act as if the now-dead friendships didn't bother me, as if I wasn't deeply hurt and mourning the one friendship I cared about. But I had no confidence to confront the issue.

On that sunny May graduation day, I was met with fake "congrats" from those old friends who felt distant and unheartfelt—it was "have to" energy, not genuine.

I remember hugging Scott, the one I married in fifth grade, the one who stole his mother's ring, the one who ditched his class to ride in my car as I ran an errand for another teacher, the one I sat next to in English class, laughing over the stupidest stuff we would come up with. I reached my arms above his tall shoulders to squeeze this person who had brought me joy during my hardest school year.

A flood of emotion came over me—a need to know what he did with the rest of his life. I thought in my head, "I can't wait to see where he goes in his life, and I wish him so much happiness."

I thought it was because we had shared some good laughs.

I didn't know it was because I was to become his wife.

The Lesson

I never knew the intertwining of plans God had in store for me.

I know now that when you have put sincerity and time into a relationship, when you've been a good, honest, caring, loving friend (although not perfect—who is?), and the friendship still tanks—you weren't meant to continue with those people. God had other friends and another direction He was pulling you toward.

I couldn't see it. Again, I was too far in.

In high school, I didn't know that letting go of those friendships would bring great clarity to the sincere, honest, equal friendships I would gain—the kind that don't ask you to be someone you are not.

It is hard to embrace change and hold the pose when relationships are changing. I have learned that if they are fizzling out, it is for a reason. I will no longer people-please my way into maintaining friendships.

True Friendship Means Equal Pouring

We equally pour out from the depths of our goodness, kindness, and even challenging and heartfelt moments. If I had continued gripping onto friends I wasn't meant to stay with, I wouldn't have had room for the ones God brought into my life.

The Three Friendship Spectrums

I now classify people into three friendship spectrums, understanding these will help you know where to invest your energy and what to expect from each level.

Acquaintance Friends – Those you don't see often. You do a surface-level catch-up each time you see them: "How's the family?" "Oh, good." Facebook friends also fall into this category—people you have known for a long time—but they don't have your phone number.

Inner Circle Friends – These are the friends you do life with, the ones your kids have activities with, and the families who get together to grill while the kids play. You're experiencing life with them. They are on your phone, you text them and get together often, yet they don't know the deep crevices of your heart because something inside doesn't allow it or trust them with that intimate knowledge. This will be your largest group of friends.

Heart Friends – This is an elite members-only club. It takes a long time to make your way into it, and it offers the deepest level of being seen, heard, and supported. It isn't perfect, but you have deep trust in that person's intention—even if there is a misunderstanding, you know it will get fixed. Typically, only one or two spots are available for this role. You are really fortunate if you have these filled. They are your true ride-or-die bitches. They come with no judgment, yet also can snap you out of a spiral if you need it. I have the privilege of having two, and they fill my heart and show me what true sisterhood is meant to look like.

Your spouse will be the king or queen of the heart category if you allow it. They will support your deepest desires and hold you through your darkest fears.

Reflection Questions

Now that you understand the three friendship spectrums, it's time to evaluate your own friendships. Be honest about where people truly belong:

1. **Do you have a complicated friendship where you can't be yourself?** One where they don't know or wouldn't accept the real you? The kind where you have fun together, but shit, you better not say anything too crazy or they might downplay you, tell you you're crazy, or just think you are too much?

2. **Who in your life is your intuition telling you to move on from?** It might be someone you feel great with in the moment, but then when you leave, you feel like shit and don't know why. Somehow, you protect yourself within, not showing your true colors.

3. **Where do your current friendships actually fit?** Spend some time reflecting on the friendships in your life and how they fit into those categories (Acquaintance, Inner Circle, Heart). Are you treating acquaintances like heart friends? Are you expecting heart-level intimacy from inner-circle friends?

4. **Are you trauma-dumping on everyone you meet?** If you are someone who tells everyone your life story the moment you meet them, consider saving it for your heart friends or even your inner circle. Pay attention to whether you share everything with everyone and how it makes you feel afterward.

It's time to get busy and find yourself in a new room with people you are striving to calibrate toward.

Section
TWO

BREAKING
THE CHAINS

CHAPTER 11
THE PEOPLE PLEASING REALMS

Before I tell you the story in this chapter, I want to share a tool.

When you are finally aware that you are a people pleaser, that you desire more, and that you want to break free from the glass ceiling you have created, there is a tool I made to help you gauge how far you're shooting on your own journey out of people pleasing.

The Four Realms

Picture you are standing outside in a large, open field. On the far end, there is a lake; it's separated from you by about the distance of a football field. Positioned right in the center between you and the lake is a random basketball hoop. Yeah, I don't know anyone who would put a hoop out in a gorgeous open field with a lake behind it, but go with me! From where you are standing, the lake seems far away —really hard to throw a basketball into; however, halfway down the field is the hoop.

I know this is getting technical, but hang in there with me. Believe me, I am not a sports fanatic, but this visual came to me while talking with my daughter one day, and it's a great tool you can use.

When you are breaking the habits of a people pleaser, you will FEEL like a bitch, because you have been conditioned for so long that if you are not serving others, you are wrong and mean. There is a vast difference between being a bitch and feeling like a bitch. Most people's pleasers will never actually become bitchy, they will just judge and shame themselves as they step onto new paths of action and healing.

Realm One: "People-Pleasing Prison" (The current situation)

The grassy field in front of you, up to that circle, will be called "The People-Pleasing Prison"—it keeps you in the same habits. It makes you feel safe because you are so embodied in it that it feels like home, but a really dark, sad home.

When you fall back into this prison, you create no traction on gaining your authority and dominion or breaking free from the people-pleasing chains that hold you down.

Realm Two: "Caressing the Crown"

There will be a small circle called "Caressing the Crown" around the hoop. This is the zone you may land in when you are trying to find your balance and FEEL like you are being a bitch. You are shaky and nervous to speak up for yourself. You request what you need, but your tone is wobbly, and your energy is confusing to the other person.

They hear the words, but your body language does not match that powerful statement because inside you are fighting a personal battle—not actually believing you are worthy to request your desire. Therefore, you are flooded with feelings of guilt, shame, and bitchiness. You might retract your request and pull yourself back into the people-pleasing zone.

Realm Three: "Real Bitch Lake"

We are going to call the lake "Real Bitch Lake." This is when you do a full send after years of built-up resentment and not speaking up for yourself, and you have finally had enough—so much that it may go too far into being a REAL bitch move.

That's okay. Re-adjust. Mend your heart by having a conversation with that person and "clarifying that your intention was..." This helps you bridge the gap between not being the "sorry girl" and knowing your intention was important, too.

Realm Four: "Devoured with Velvet" - THE GOAL

The hoop will be named "Devoured with Velvet"—freaking nailed it, energy. Getting the ball in the hoop is the goal. This is the sweet success of not only meeting your own needs but also those of others. This is what I call "kind confidence": you are kind to others by supporting them, but confident first in meeting your needs and not bypassing to people-please.

Once you ebb and flow for a while between all the realms, you will land more frequently in realm four. It will start happening naturally, AND you will not feel like a bitch at all. You will not even know that old version of yourself.

You will embody a new version of yourself—one who can't even imagine a time when you worried so much. A version of you that holds great empathy for the time you wasted giving SO much thought to others' opinions and needs, when you see what your power really is and how you can light up the world and still help people from your overflow that never runs out.

The Woman You're Becoming

It never runs out because she knows her worth. She is connected to God and source energy. She knows when it is her time to help and when helping means letting the other person figure it out for themselves.

She is strong, brilliant, bold, courageous, soft, dark, light, receptive, fluid, deep, mysterious, creative, magnetising, embodied, feminine, masculine, edgy, fierce, and provocative.

AND she doesn't apologize for ANY of it—she OWNS every piece of herself.

Back to the Story

Relationships are a large part of this book because most of life's highs and lows revolve around them.

Post-Graduation: Engagement and Entrapment

It was after graduation, and one of my friends had gotten engaged. She was one of my older friends who had graduated before I did, the one who lived down my OGB's lane. We kept in touch as close friends. She was working and living with her now-fiancé, a man she had dated for a few years. She was happy and learning how to navigate real-life challenges in this now-serious relationship.

I wasn't one to judge, since I was still dating Zack at the time and having questionable conversations with him, too. She was in love with this man and was doing everything necessary to make it work. In that time, she had also remained friends with my now (thank goodness) ex-"convenience" friend.

After she got engaged, she immediately asked me to be her "Maid of Honor."

I was thrilled. I was just out of high school, and I couldn't believe we were going to experience something we had talked about on endless nights while applying fake nails and doing our hair as large as we could with half a bottle of Aqua Net. She had found her person.

Meanwhile, in my own relationship, things were getting more off course.

At the time, I hadn't yet gone to cosmetology school, so I was working in accounts payable for my family's gravel business. It was consistent, Monday-through-Friday, all-day work that I had left my teller job for.

It was a blessing and also a realization that I didn't want a desk job looking at numbers all day. I remember being so unbelievably bored with the work itself, and sitting on my tush all day was a hard thing for me to do.

After my friend asked me to be her maid of honor, I went to the local bookstore and bought Martha Stewart's huge wedding-planning book. I surprised my friend with it and some other fun wedding celebration gifts!

She had asked my old "convenience friend" to be at her wedding as well, but it didn't matter. I knew I would show up and support the bride.

Until one day.

The House of Cards

A few months into the planning process, it was all coming to a head. The years of my confidence were long gone at this point. I worried about everything. I questioned the relationships around me and felt as though I was standing on an unstable house of cards that I had built.

I had built it for myself by not breaking up with a guy who mind-fucked me into submission and doubt of everything I had loved in my life, just so he could keep me around to borrow money from that well-paying, consistent job I had.

I had built it by giving up on the joys of my life and not riding my horse, but a few times a year now.

I had built it by continuing to give him money, paying for most of our dinner dates, and saving so we could go to Vegas for my birthday.

He added nothing.

Again, we go back to why I stayed with him. If you have ever been with a manipulative person, they know how to play your strings so well that it feels impossible. He would reel me in or do something good right as he thought I had my foot out the door.

Also—hi, remember me, people pleaser extraordinaire? I didn't know who the heck I was. I was too busy making sure everyone else in my life was happy. I would get home from work, and instead of going out to ride my horse or do something for myself, I would stay inside, waiting for the phone to ring so I could talk to my boyfriend.

Ick. Thinking of that now makes me cringe.

Cell phones were becoming a thing as we were dating, and I spent too many hours waiting inside, afraid of missing his call. He would do whatever he wanted, and we wouldn't be able to talk on the phone as I had hoped. Dumb, I know, but at the time it was real.

When I got a cell phone, and I was out of high school, I would drive around town, killing time, waiting for him to say it was a good time to meet up.

I wasted so much freaking time waiting on that asshole.

Why? Because, as a people pleaser, I had ZERO boundaries. I didn't even know what a boundary was.

So there I was—a shell of a person I didn't recognize anymore—and my house of cards felt wobbly in multiple ways.

My relationship that I had committed to for years now felt questionable and problematic. Yet I felt stuck, unable to change anything or lift my feet from the ground to move in a new direction. My friendships had dissolved, except for this one bride. I didn't know what I wanted to do in life, and I had stopped riding my beloved horses.

Basically, I was incredibly insecure and a fraction of who I was meant to be or had been years prior.

A few odd things had happened, making me question whether my friend actually wanted me as her maid of honor. The door to doubt had been creaking open, and one day it was fully blown off the hinges.

The Breaking Point

I was right in the middle of the busiest week in accounts payable when my engaged friend asked me to go dress shopping with her in a neighboring town.

I had supported her and indulged her with gifts and goodies to help with the excitement and support of her wedding. Listened with a supportive ear to any worries or doubts she had about the upcoming events. I had given and given, and I desperately wanted to watch as this friend tried on wedding gowns for her big day.

She asked if I could go on a particular day that week, and I apologized and told her I couldn't. I actually asked my boss (my mom) at the time, and she confirmed we were too busy that week and needed all hands on deck. My hands were tied—I couldn't quit my job to take a day to look at gowns.

I offered the next week or two of options. I could spend the whole day helping her pick out her dress.

She said no. Her mind was made up. (Rightfully so—it was her wedding, and she was the only one necessary to be there.)

Have no fear—the "convenience friend" snuck in again and gladly took my spot. Without batting an eye, they went without me.

There had been a few things that had been done that should've been my duty, and the "convenience friend" placed herself into the role if I wasn't available. I also had real-life responsibilities at the time, but she wasn't willing to find a time I could join her. She was just happy and excited to go pick out her dress.

So they went. Without me.

I don't blame the bride at all, looking back. She was so freaking excited. She had the day off, and she was going to find her dress.

However, that was the final straw that broke the insecure, doubting camel's back in my heart.

The Full Send to "Real Bitch Lake"

I was done. I was done fighting for my importance in friendships. I was done trying to intermingle with this old "convenience" friend because she was a bossy force, and I, at the time, couldn't muster the nerve to reclaim my territory.

I snapped.

I was SO hurt. I did the responsible thing that day: I went to my job, did the accounts payable work. But I was steaming inside, teary all day, and then angry as hell.

It wasn't just about the dress or that day specifically. It was years of pouring out my power to other friends and receiving a fraction back, and the dam finally broke. All the water and memories came flooding in as a force that couldn't be reckoned with.

The door to doubt was off the hinges, and insecurity was the paint scheme that surrounded me. In my heart, this day confirmed that I wasn't actually desired to be the maid of honor—because most brides want the maid of honor to be part of their special day, picking out the dress we had dreamed of and talking about doing together for five-plus years.

I arrived home after a long day, and my sadness had turned into anger.

Imagine that field with the lake and the hoop again. Imagine the hoop is half the distance between you and the lake. Our goal when breaking people-pleasing habits is to aim for the hoop and make a swish.

Well, that day I grew extra muscle as the dam broke, and all the built-up frustration came pouring out.

I aimed, and I effing threw that ball right into "Real Bitch Lake." It didn't even blink an eye as I left the "People-Pleasing Prison." I sailed past "Caressing the Crown" and "Devoured with Velvet," and it landed deep into "Real Bitch Lake."

I did a full send.

What is this action I did?

I called my engaged friend mid-evening, after convincing myself all day and for several weeks leading up to this point that she didn't want me to be her maid of honor and that she wanted this "convenience" friend instead, and she didn't know how to tell me.

So I dialed her number, and told her I was de-throning myself, taking off my maid-of-honor crown, and that she could give it to the "convenience friend."

She was shocked, as most people would be. She was crying. I was crying. She pleaded that even if I weren't the maid of honor, she wouldn't give the position to the "convenience" friend.

I didn't believe her. My house of cards was falling.

I was literally setting a torch to the last of the five in the friendship group I had been so close with for seven years.

That day was one of the hardest of my life, friendship-wise.

As I hung up the phone, I bawled for days. I had just ruined a friendship over years of people-pleasing, and the dam holding it all together finally broke. It broke a friendship that, at the time, I thought shouldn't have been broken.

Hindsight is 20/20. I was meant to move on.

God had slowly weaseled the other friends out of my people-pleasing clutches, but He was waiting for me to find the torch inside, to also participate in what I was creating and desiring in life, to step up and take action. He could only help so far, and then it was up to me to make the action around my desires.

That day, I found the torch and burned to the ground the remaining cliquey friendships I had built. That day, I found the courage and a glimpse of strength—misled, yes, but still strength. That day, I realized I could do a full send into "Real Bitch Lake." It just took years and years of build-up for the dam to break.

A Full-Circle Moment

I will always hold this friend with deep love and care. She was doing what she wanted to do to celebrate and plan her big day.

Of course, as a people-pleaser, I carried this guilt for years. Years later, we spoke again, and she was even at my wedding. I don't know how—that was true strength and compassion from her. We both put up boundaries after that and no longer speak.

Even now, when we have a rare opportunity to be in a room together, we don't acknowledge the other; it's not sad—it's just a new normal.

I know, with no doubt in my heart, that I was meant to change the path of my friendships. I was meant to break the cliquishness of small-town friendships for myself, and I was meant to fully break wide open and re-create a new life and path.

When I see the community she has surrounded herself with, I am so grateful God sent me in a different direction. I would not be the person I am today if I had gotten stuck on that path.

Although we do not speak, and I wouldn't choose to be in that circle she has created, I send all my love, care, and joy to her and the life she has created for herself.

The Lesson

When you have been a people pleaser for so long, it will build up, and you are likely to have a full-send moment into "Real Bitch Lake."

It is your way out. It may only take one time, but it will calibrate you and liberate you even when it feels like full shame.

If you don't know how deep the lake is, how do you know if you can jump or walk in? Sometimes we have to let it all go to realize where the balance lies.

Gauging Your Aim

The goal is to catch yourself each time as you are breaking free from "People-Pleasing Prison." Ask yourself:

- Did I have a full-send moment into "Real Bitch Lake" and go too far?

- Did I throw it in my mind but didn't speak up, keeping myself stuck in the "People-Pleasing Prison"?

- Did I send it, but it didn't quite land right? Your energy doesn't match your words, confusing people and putting you in "Caressing the Crown." You are close to your intentions, but you stepped out and were brave yet not embodied.

- Or did you freaking nail it? Finding your kind confidence, stating your needs in power while also acknowledging someone else's needs, swishing the ball in the hoop, and placing you right into "Devoured with Velvet."

Reflection Questions

Now that you understand the Four Realms, it's time to assess where you are and where you're aiming:

1. **Where are you aiming right now?** Which realm are you currently living in most of the time?

2. **Have you ever had a full-send moment into "Real Bitch Lake"?** What happened? Did it liberate you, or did you retreat back to the prison?

3. **Are you stuck in the "People-Pleasing Prison" and have never even tried to break free?** What's keeping you there? Fear? Guilt? The belief that you don't have permission to change?

4. **Have you landed in "Caressing the Crown"?** That shaky place where you wanted to send it but couldn't find your footing and ended up feeling like a bitch? You're close, my love. Keep going.

5. **Have you ever had a moment—a glimpse—of the sweet spot?** The balance, the swishing of the hoop in "Devoured with Velvet," finding your kind confidence? Where can you speak your truth without even an itch of trembling?

A Promise

I promise you it is possible not only to go there but to stay there. Because from "Devoured with Velvet," you then pour from the overflow you are now dripping with. You are able to stay true to yourself and speak your mind while also loving others.

CHAPTER 12
TINY STEPS

The few months following my "full send" outburst left me feeling ripped wide open in a way I hadn't ever felt. I wasn't fully living in the path I desired, but I had started contemplating what was next, which shifted my perspective enough to declare that I wanted something other than this number-crunching desk job.

I remembered meeting a woman at the teller counter who was so unbelievably passionate about her salon and her life as a cosmetologist. I made an appointment at her salon to get a glimpse of what that lifestyle was like. I couldn't get an appointment with her, but I knew it would help if I could immerse myself in some of the energy radiating out of her—energy flowing as complete adoration for her job. I had my hair cut there a few times and spoke with the cosmetologists about their lifestyle and employment. It sounded really nice: not going into work until nine, getting to move around, standing most of the day, listening to fun music, being creative, and having fun girly conversations while making someone else feel beautiful. Yes, please!

That was the polar opposite of sitting all day, looking at numbers, and having conversations with construction men in my pink shirts and girly demeanor. I had both sides pulsing heavily through my veins, and I knew my time with a desk job for the construction company wasn't what I was desiring any longer. I wanted to try my hand at a pair of scissors. The coolest part is that this woman led a small cosmetology program out of her salon. It was an investment in schooling, but I was excited about the lifestyle and to apply myself in a new creative way.

Up to this point, I had taken a couple of business classes at a local business college and disliked them. My mind found it so dull that I wanted to come out of my skin, so I stopped taking them, feeling lost on my path again, until I found this salon.

The Gentleman Who Reminded Me of Scott

While I was waiting for my cosmetology classes to begin, I was wrapping up my time working in accounts payable at the family business. I would often pass people coming and going from the real estate company downstairs. There was this tall, slender gentleman who must have had the same lunch hour as me, because I saw him a few steps ahead of me each time I returned from lunch and walked through the parking lot. We said hi a few times, and I couldn't stop pondering who he reminded me of. I couldn't put my finger on it for a couple of weeks, but then it hit me hard.

He reminded me of Scott, the guy at graduation whom I hugged and wondered what he would do with his life. His mannerisms, his dark hair slightly laced with red, and the light freckles on his face reminded me of Scott, grown up.

I saw Scott once after graduation; he had been working at an auto parts store while attending the local college. We said a quick hello and caught up for a few minutes. He had informed me he was leaving at the end of the summer to join the Marine Corps. After that talk, I went on about my life and let it fade into a distant memory until this gentleman brought Scott back to the forefront of my mind.

Scott and I had a mutual friend that we shared while growing up—her name was Hanna—and I knew she probably kept in touch with him. It had probably been about a year since I had run into him, and my curiosity was percolating. What had happened with him? Each time I saw this other gentleman at work, it brought back memories of laughing with him in English class our senior year and his easygoing nature.

I let it sit for a few days, then reached out to Hanna to see if she knew where he was. She was up in the northern part of the state attending college. I emailed to see how life was going for her and ended by asking if she knew where Scott was at this time. When she replied, she included a mailing address to a Marine Corps base located in California.

The Pink Perfume Letter

I was delighted to hear so many things were going well for my friend Hanna; she was enjoying college and had met the man she would marry and go on to have many adorable children with. I was also curiously flirting with the idea of sending a note to this address. He was a friend, a genuine friend, and I wanted to check in on how his life was going.

Remember how I liked pink? Well, guess what—I had a rainbow stash of stationery colors, and pink was one of them, so of course I used it. I wrote a simple one- to two-page letter, saying hello, asking what he was up to and how things were going, and updating him on my life, which at the time was about to shift to cosmetology school. I thought it was a great idea to spray the letter with perfume. Why? I have no idea. It seemed like something to do when you are twenty years old and have just watched Legally Blonde. I hadn't thought of him as a potential boyfriend, but I wanted it to be special and different from the mail he most likely received.

I was still dating Zack, and the tank of gas in our relationship was running out. The gas light had come on, and I was driving without giving a shit about pulling over to fill it up. I was at the end, running on fumes, and I was willing to let it die. I wasn't, by any means, reaching out to Scott with romantic intentions; instead, I felt divine guidance to check in on a friend. The idea of going to cosmetology had lit up a center of excitement and passion I hadn't felt for a while, and I wanted to spread some cheer.

I sent the letter, quit my number-crunching desk job, and started a nine-month cosmetology program.

Cosmetology School

I heard nothing back from the letter, moved on to the path in front of me, and was having so much fun in the salon. I love the energy of the salon; it has its own vibe. A buzz of ladies yelling over hair dryers and bee-bopping around, knowing they were helping other people feel better about themselves. School was held in a tiny room above the salon, so although I didn't have my own chair, I could feel the energy bumping downstairs. I loved it!

Over time, I studied and practiced on my manikin and eventually started taking students. I was so nervous and definitely messed up a few times—whoops, sorry to those few out there. I didn't get your layers correct. That wasn't fun, and I felt horrible. I had messed up someone's hair, and I would be "that" hairdresser they talk about from that one terrible haircut. The people pleaser in me ached when that happened, but I had to march forward. I learned that the angle I used was wrong and did it better next time—after, of course, ten million apologies to the girl whose hair I messed up, leaving shelves of layers in her thick, long, luscious locks.

I did get the hang of it, and I still cut a few family members' hair now, one with long layers, and multiple people want to come to me for the same cut. But that chapter of my life experience is closed, so I gratefully decline new clients.

The DMV Moment

I was about halfway through my program, and it was the beginning of May. I was really starting to enjoy the idea of becoming a cosmetologist soon, especially with the added bonus that most salons are closed on Mondays, which meant I could run errands on a day when most people were at work. I was headed in on my day off to a naturopath appointment, and I remembered my vehicle registration was due soon. I had some extra time, so

I decided to stop in and pay to renew my tags. I walked into the DMV, and everything was flowing in my direction. They immediately called my number and sent me right back to my clerk. When does that ever happen in a DMV?

I knew the lady I would be speaking with, Nancy, as I had spent a lot of time on the phone with her, working on my family's business and handling equipment and truck registrations. I saw Nancy, walked past the people standing at the counter for the driver's license renewals, and took care of my tags. I thanked her after we spent a few minutes chit-chatting, then turned around and started walking toward the exit.

My hand was about to touch the handle when I heard "Rachel." I thought nothing of it, whirled around to see who was beckoning my name, and there stood Scott—yes, the one I wrote my pink perfume letter to. The Scott that I hugged on graduation day, knowing I wasn't ready to let him go, the one who had made me laugh over and over in English class, and even the one that I married on the playground in fifth grade.

Except he looked different now. In high school, and when I saw him a year or two ago, he was a 6'1" string bean basketball player who weighed 140 lbs of lean muscle. Standing in front of me at this moment was a freaking beast—the Hulk compared—clearly the workings of the military and many days in the gym and eating MREs. My brain couldn't compute that this was him.

I had always put him in the friend zone, but when I saw him standing there looking like a sexy gladiator Marine, he shattered through the brick wall of the friend zone into holy shit, he's so handsome land! His gaze was intense, like a lion locked onto its prey, ready to delve into my soul with its piercing blue eyes.

It took me a second to realize it was Scott, and then I greeted him with a cheery hello and a hug, which was hard to wrap my arms around his enlarged muscles. He finished renewing his driver's license, which had nearly expired while he was serving in Iraq on his first deployment, and then told me he was home for two weeks on military leave, spending time with his dad. It was perfect timing, as his birthday was a hard one to forget—Cinco de Mayo—and it was a couple of days away. I asked him if I could take him to lunch while he was in town to celebrate his birthday, and he agreed. We exchanged numbers and scheduled it for a few days away.

Lunch, Emails, and Breaking Free

I met him for lunch a couple of days later. I had told my fizzling-out boyfriend that I would be having lunch with this friend; little did I know that Scott and I would relate and laugh about a new common ground: being in a relationship with people we no longer saw going anywhere. We had a lot to catch up on, sitting and laughing for hours next to a window in a restaurant while people buzzed by in the small mountain town I lived in. Neither of us noticed, as it was pure delight to connect with a friend again.

It was time for me to leave, so we exchanged email addresses, since email was still a very popular form of communication back then. We hugged and went our separate ways. I was going back to school, and he was headed back to California, where he was stationed. We ended up writing emails to each other throughout that summer, and I learned a lot about what he was doing, and he listened to my excitement about being almost done with this schooling and stepping into this new career.

I was nearing the end of my time as a student and studying for the boards. I wanted to do well in my written and practical exams. Things were shifting inside me as I attended the school I desired. I was gaining confidence—confidence that I could do something for myself and commit to it, no matter the hours and dedication it would take. Rather than waiting around for my boyfriend to call, I was taking tiny steps toward what I wanted.

I had tried three times to break up with him that summer, again, the master manipulator, and I finally pulled the band-aid off and found the sweet spot of the "Devoured in Velvet" stage. I didn't waver; instead, I was steady, strong, and kind. He knew he had a good run, and it was finally over. He tried a few more times to get back together and would stalk me at work, to the point that my dad had to intervene to get the hint—although it wouldn't entirely stop until a little later in the story.

I was stepping onto a new path: I had broken up with my boyfriend of nearly five years. I felt free, wild, and happy. I passed the boards with flying colors, and I was starting to build a real clientele in my new salon career.

The Lesson

I learned to follow those nudges of curiosity and take baby steps, because when you are a people pleaser, it feels huge to consider possibly letting someone else down. I didn't want to let my mom down when I told her I wouldn't be the third generation of bookkeepers in our family business. It was hard, but I stepped onto that ledge of curiosity, led by a new desire: to enjoy what I do.

It took a few tries to break up with Zack, but each time I grew stronger, knowing what my wording needed to be, and then I held the pose. It took saying yes to something less scary, so I could build my confidence one step at a time, knowing that breaking up with him would be hard. But the words and holding the pose were the only complex parts; my soul felt set free once I drove away from Zack that day—not because of him, but because I finally listened to the inner voice and realigned with my path and purpose.

Reflection Questions

Take some time to sit with these questions. Journal your responses. Be honest, raw, and kind with yourself.

1. **Where are you fighting against a nudge, curiosity, or joy because you feel so stuck and afraid to move a muscle?** Do you feel like the house of cards will crumble under you?

2. **What if they did?** And what if it was the best thing that ever happened to you?

3. **What tiny step could you take today toward something that lights you up—even if it feels scary or like you might let someone down?**

4. **Where have you been waiting for permission to follow your own desires?** What would it feel like to give yourself that permission right now?

CHAPTER 13
DELICIOUS DESIRE

The Feeling I Couldn't Shake

I couldn't shake the feeling, the nudge, the little curiosity around my excitement and joy each time I would see an email from Scott. We never spoke on the phone; it was just letters anticipating what he might say next. I could feel my heart race each time I thought of him, and I giggled over the funny comments he made in the emails I received.

I was confused. I had never thought of him as a potential date because he never showed that side of himself to me, but now, after all our shared words, I was starting to feel something, and those feelings came with confusion. In late August, I got the gumption to email him to ask if he would be coming back to see his dad anytime soon, because I would love to see him in person again. I knew I needed to be in his presence to see whether I was making these feelings up or if they were true desires of my heart.

Labor Day Leave

To my surprise, he emailed right back and said he was coming in a week or two for Labor Day leave and had a 96-hour reprieve that would allow him to be off base. He wanted to see his dad, but it wasn't until later that he revealed he was having the same thoughts about me and wanted to see me in person.

We arranged to meet at a park in town, as he and his buddy—weirdly, stationed together yet from the same small mountain town—rolled in after a 12-hour nonstop drive. I would drive him to his father's house, where he would spend the next three nights. On the way to his dad's, he asked if I was available the next day to go miniature golfing and grab lunch. I, of course, agreed, since we only had about thirty minutes to his dad's house, and that wouldn't be enough time to tell if I was making up feelings or starting to develop something tangible.

I met his dad for the first time that night. I only stayed for about 30 minutes because I knew he wanted time alone with his son; however, an odd thing happened during those 30 minutes. His dad asked me, in Scott's place, if I would go to the Marine Corps Ball with his son in November. It was an odd situation for a dad to be asking a girl to a ball for his son, so my reply was, "Well, Kenny, thank you; however, I will allow your son to ask me if he really wants me to go." We all laughed, and I could tell Scott was deeply embarrassed.

The Parking Lot Confession

The next day, I met him in town, we were coming from different directions, and it hadn't been clarified that it was a date, just a friendly hangout. We met in the parking lot of an electric company my father worked for because I knew I could leave my vehicle there safely. I climbed into his dad's big Dodge, which he was driving because he had ridden with his friend from California and didn't have his own truck here.

We drove to a popular BBQ restaurant that also had a miniature golf course out back. He parked the truck, and as I reached for the door handle to open my door and climb out, he said, "Wait," so I lowered my hand and leaned back in my seat.

"Are you ok?" I asked him. He wasn't looking at me, and his energy had changed. He stated that he needed to tell me something.

"Ok, can you look at me or take off your sunglasses?" I replied, as this seemed really serious and intense.

"No," he answered.

"Okay, go ahead, I'll listen," trying to help him become comfortable with what seemed to be something challenging to say.

Well, it was. I watched as he stepped into one of the bravest things I had seen a guy my age do up until that point. We sat in the truck for the next 30 minutes as he confessed his love for me, which had been developing since the first time he saw me in second grade. To say I was baffled would be an understatement.

I will leave out a lot of our conversation for our privacy; however, I learned in those thirty minutes as he stepped outside his comfort zone and showed bold bravery, that I wasn't the only one developing feelings. He had crushed on me for years, and he would be honored to have me on his arm at the Marine Corps Ball.

I was stunned. I didn't know what to say. Of course, I said yes to the ball—I mean, heck yeah—it sounded fun, and I wanted to be with him! But the rest of what he said was bouncing around in my head like a kid wound up on sugar, not knowing where to begin their focus. I had no idea. He was so unbelievably shy that he had never said a thing; the rumor had never made it to me that he cared for me in that way.

Looking back, I see little things that cued me in; however, a girl cannot assume when the other person hasn't put that information forward and made it clear. At the end of high school, he also had a girlfriend, a girl he thought he couldn't do better, even though they weren't a good match, which left him feeling stuck. Yet his family had heard about me for years around the table, and they thought he made me up because they had never met me. They encouraged him to ask me out, but he put me on a pedestal. He didn't think he could reach me until he found his confidence doing hard shit like joining the Marine Corps and going off to fight in the war after 9/11.

He, too, had to rip off the band-aids that had covered his confidence for many years. He did. He went into the Marine Corps and came out a God-fearing man who would be brave or die trying. He was a different person, and his confidence was such a turn-on!

Three Days of Bliss

He lit me up in a way no other guy could. It wasn't just his looks—of course, that helped—it was his mannerisms, his confidence, his "I don't give a shit attitude," but "I want you" laser focus. Our conversations just rolled; we never stopped talking and laughing. He lit up parts of me I didn't even know I had, and I wanted more. He got another shot at asking me to be his; he stepped into that alignment with shaky confidence, and the pieces fell perfectly into place.

After that talk, I knew what I had been feeling wasn't misguided; I knew it was right, aligned with where my path was going. We spent the day together and basically planned out the rest of the weekend. I spent the days with him, and he spent the nights with his dad. We had a connection unlike anything I had ever experienced. Every time the other one spoke, we listened with deep intention, hanging on every word in pure indulgent curiosity, as though the other one were giving life-or-death instructions.

I couldn't take my focus off his eyes and chiseled jaw; he was so handsome, big, strong, funny, intelligent, and self-led. I was having an out-of-body experience compared to what I had been through in a previous relationship. So different that after we ate dinner one night, we were walking to the truck when he started walking to the passenger side. I crossed over and started heading to the driver's side. He stopped, looked at me, and said, "What are you doing?"

I replied, "Did you want me to drive?"

He looked baffled. "No, I was opening the door for you," he stated slowly.

Oh, my goodness, yes, boys had opened the door for me in the past, but I had been in a relationship for so long that didn't subscribe to gentlemanly behaviors. It truly confused me. We laughed, and I realized how Twilight Zone this situation really was.

By the end of those three days, my stomach hurt from laughing, and we had strangers approach us, telling us they loved watching us interact at our table. I felt so connected to this person, and he just seemed to get me. On that last day together, I had my second, first kiss with him that ended our weekend of bliss.

The Lesson

I had an urge that prompted my intuition to ask, "Can I see you in person soon?" I asked for something I desired, not knowing if the other person was willing or able. Yet they were, and if I hadn't ever asked, where would it have gone? Where would we be now?

As people pleasers, we are so conditioned not to ask for what we desire. We're taught that asking is unsafe, that we are too much. Yet some of life's most significant gifts are met when you ask for what your heart is calling for.

Reflection Questions

Take some time to sit with these questions. Journal your responses. Be honest, raw, and kind with yourself.

1. **Do you have a burning desire that you are too afraid to ask for?** What is it? Write it down.

2. **What are the worst things that could happen if you asked?** Maybe you ask someone out, and they turn you down—will you burst into flames? No. You will know it is time to move on.

3. **What are the desires of your heart that need to be spoken out loud, even if they feel scary?** List them. Say them aloud to yourself.

4. **Where in your life have you been waiting for permission or a sign before asking for what you truly want?** What would it feel like to stop waiting and just ask?

CHAPTER 14
THROUGH A NEW LENS

The Marine Corps Ball Weekend

It was November, and I flew to California for the Marine Corps Ball. My mom and I had found a beautiful dress that called to me. Although white—most women wore anything but white at the ball—I didn't care; that is what my heart wanted. I have family in San Diego, where the ball would be held, and he had family north of LA. We decided to make a whole weekend out of the adventure and go to the ball, spend some time at his family's house, and some time at my family's home, getting to know everyone. It was a whirlwind.

The first night I arrived, he picked me up at the airport, and we headed to my aunt's house. It was late in the evening. I had young cousins, and she had already put them to bed. By the time we arrived, the house was dark, and she quietly showed us where to go—that was after I called on the landline, probably waking everyone up because we were lost. She had offered to give me directions, but I have one of those memories that I can remember a path and road if I have been on it once. Apparently, it had been too long, and things looked different at night. So we tiptoed to our room, trying not to wake everyone up again.

We whispered for the next few hours, which I am sure my aunt could hear through the walls of her early-1900s beach bungalow; it's such a fabulous home, however, not soundproof. I am sure she was annoyed having two small children trying to sleep, but she kindly never mentioned it.

The Ball

The next day was the ball, and we went to a gorgeous hotel in the bay of downtown San Diego. It was the fanciest hotel I had ever been to, and it felt so unusual for a small-town country girl to dress up in any form of a fancy gown. We checked into the hotel, and I was so nervous—I was like a little kid with anxiety and excitement about getting on a roller coaster. This was maxing out my nervous system for sure. I wondered, could I trust him? Was he really a good guy? Those thoughts were then being met with "duh, you grew up with him. This isn't Joe Blow." That would calm me down and let me enjoy this special occasion.

I had just turned twenty-two, and he was just a few months older. This felt so grown-up and surreal again for my country-cowgirl, small-town heart that had never experienced anything so fancy. He looked so dashing in his Blues, fitted just right and accentuating his ripped frame, his jawline strong and sharp, his eyes still making me slightly uncomfortable as I got lost in the deep ocean-blue stare. I felt like a Twilight Belle stepping into another reality of possibility.

The ball proceeded; we ate a delicious, beautiful dinner in a dimly lit room; the music began, and multiple hip-thrusting, get-down-and-dirty songs came on. I was out of my element. I was a country dancer—a two-stepping, line-dancing, swinging girl. Although my mom and I loved to dance wildly to good old-time Rock 'n' Roll classics, bump-and-grind music had me panicking, looking for the door, wanting to bolt like a stampede of horses.

I watched as Scott went out and danced with the crowd for one song. Don't get me wrong, this girl LOVES to dance, and now I will dance to anything, but back then, in this reality illusion, I didn't feel one iota comfortable bumping and grinding. He did. I saw him move his hips in a way that no other guy I had dated seemed to be capable of. I watched in awe at his confidence and "no eff's given" attitude, smiling in delight the entire time. The next song started, and he invited me to the floor. I went, and for a moment started dancing that way, and then froze. He leaned in and whispered, "Do you want to go somewhere else?"

Heavens, yes, anywhere, I thought, but instead said, "Yes, please."

We gathered our few items and, while the music was raging, we slipped out the door into the lobby and down the hall to a beautiful hotel bar. I hadn't enjoyed cocktails yet, but we ordered a glass of wine and stared into each other's eyes as we talked for hours. I will never forget a gentleman who paid respect to Scott in his uniform, saying kind words as he bought our drinks.

Meeting His Family

The next day, we drove a couple of hours to his sister's house north of LA, where I was met with warmth and kindness as I was introduced to his older sister, her husband, their two kids—he had two nephews; one was about five, and the other was three months old—and also his mother, who was living with them at the time. They lived in a beautiful, large home with a gorgeous view on the edge of wine country. They were so unbelievably welcoming and confirmed his story, which he told me a few months back: they didn't know if I was real, but they had heard of me weekly for years.

It was enlightening. His sister was a fantastic cook, and we spent a lot of time laughing and learning about each other that evening. The next morning, we hugged them goodbye and drove back to my aunt's house in San Diego.

We enjoyed a night out with them, where I had too many drinks for a person who didn't drink alcohol often and had to leave the restaurant early due to our pre-party—which was filled with a couple of vodka Red Bulls.

Yeah, for a girl who didn't drink hard alcohol or energy drinks, that was a recipe for disaster. The Red Bull gave me so much energy that I hadn't realized how the vodka had set in. Once we arrived at the restaurant, I knew I wasn't ok. I asked my uncle, who was driving, if he could take me back to his house, so he dropped Scott and me off and went back to the friends they were meeting with.

Let's just say Scott got to see a part of me I didn't even know I was capable of—the "I have been drinking too much, I am now throwing up" part of me. He didn't care; he was so supportive, and I was MORTIFIED. I couldn't believe this was one of his first experiences dating me, and it hasn't happened since, nor have I ever had another Red Bull vodka. I thought he would run for the hills, that he would witness that and for sure think, "I'm out."

SeaWorld and the Decision

The next day, we had scheduled for him and me to go meander around SeaWorld before I flew home. We had some life experiences together that weekend, and now seemed to be on the fast track after years of the slow-to-no track.

It was the end of the day, and we were sitting in the 3D IMAX theater at SeaWorld waiting for that show to begin. All I could feel was bliss. I just loved being in his presence. I loved how he made me feel and the way I lit him up in return. I enjoyed being in a larger city, something I had never experienced firsthand. The reality was I was headed back to the small country town and leaving this fun weekend. I couldn't unsee the thing staring right at me. I had told people growing up that if I ever moved, I would want to go to San Diego, close to my aunt, to try it out first. We had visited many times growing up, and although there were way too many people for my liking, I wanted it to be the place I tried first, leaving a small town.

So there we were, imagining how we would have to say goodbye and not know when we would see each other again. I knew it would be hard and that there would be many months in between. Long-distance relationships are doable, but no one said they were easy. I couldn't unsee what my heart and head kept saying, so as we were talking in the theater waiting for it to begin, I blurted out, "I'm going to move to San Diego."

He was shocked. His eyes widened, and he said, "Really," with excitement and doubt arising in his voice simultaneously.

"Yes, I have always said I wanted to try it here if I moved, and I have nothing holding me there. I am so ready for a new adventure."

Suddenly, we both had peace come over us and an excitement that brought us back into the present moment and took away the edge of sadness, knowing we would need to hug goodbye in a few hours. I remember him standing in the security line with me and my leopard print luggage, clutching at the last minute. I wasn't sad. I wasn't scared. I was exhilarated to go home and plan out my next move.

Coming Home

My mom and dad eagerly awaited my story when I got home late that night. The last thing they expected was the bomb I placed on their hearts as the last topic. I discussed everything that had happened, and we giggled in delight over the things I had experienced. As the last point, I made clear that I was ready—ready to move to another state, ready to go all in on the unknown, ready to leap—and I meant it.

Remember, pure optimist. We don't think about what could go wrong; we are delusional in our confidence that things will work out. I was left with no choice; that trip had altered my reality. I couldn't unsee it. I was forever changed. I had stepped into a new identity, and there wasn't any looking back. I had calibrated to another way of living, and nothing would slow me down.

I sat there in my parents' brightly lit den telling them I wanted to move in January, which was two months away. At this time, my confidence had just started to rebuild. I felt like a crimson sparrow with small amounts of confidence, but it was fiery and fierce, ready to spread my wings and fly even if I didn't know how. I can't imagine what my parents were feeling as they crawled into bed that night, but I felt unshackled and resurgent.

The Lesson

This was the first time I put myself in such a transformative weekend—a comfortable situation, and yet so unbelievably jarring to return to reality. I couldn't do it. It was more uncomfortable in my body to go back to the way things used to be than to rise to the intimidating path that lay ahead of me. I didn't wait, like I had with most everything else in my life, waiting, as a people pleaser, for others to "approve" of this choice. Something came over me, and I couldn't even hear it if someone did say something negative about the move. I tuned it out because I DECIDED to move quickly. I didn't wait for all the worries and concerns to come up, and for fear to derail me. I had looked through a new lens and couldn't unsee the new path.

Reflection Questions

Once you see through a new lens, there's no going back. These questions will help you identify your own transformative moments and what you did—or didn't do—with them.

1. **When was a time that you were put into a situation that gave you a new perspective, even if small?** What did you see differently?

2. **Were you able to look away, or did you feel the faint siren call to answer that next level?**

3, **Did you take it, or did you return to the comfort of your current reality?** If you returned, what pulled you back?

4. **Are you still thinking about it, but you waited too long, and fear set in?** What would it look like to move on now, even if you can't find all the perfect pieces?

CHAPTER 15
QUANTUM LEAP

This was a quantum leap, a leap that changed every part of me; it changed my location, my living quarters, my shopping stores, my comfort and proximity to the family I had grown up with, my job, and on and on. I was absolutely going to become a new person because everything around me had changed, except my physical self and the clothes I wore. These are some of the best ways to completely uplevel yourself—making big, bold moves, making moves that you are excited about, yet they scare the shit out of you.

Looking back now, my eyes widen with amazement at how young I was when I took these bold risks. Hello again, it's me, the embodied optimist. There was something inside me that told me it would all work out. I moved to California with little to no savings, no job, and no apartment. Yes, you read that correctly.

First off, it was a different time, and the neighborhood I was moving to was constantly filled with apartments for rent, according to my aunt, so I had faith it would be easy to find a place to live. I was moving to a large city where more jobs would be available. We packed all my belongings into a small U-Haul trailer, and my mom and dad helped me make the very long drive to San Diego. They, of course, would want to be there; they wanted to see where I was and if I was going to be safe.

I arrived late that evening at a family member's house, who was going to let us stay there for the week while I looked for housing and work. There was no other plan but to succeed; it wasn't even a thought that I wouldn't. It was pure blind trust, as I genuinely believed I would find a place to live and a job both in one week before my parents had to go home.

The Job Hunt

The first day we got there, I submitted a resume to one of those hiring agencies that finds people and staffs them for other companies. I couldn't use my cosmetology license, which I had just spent all that time on, because California required more hours to practice legally than my home state did. I had an interview scheduled with the staffing agency that day so they could get to know me and my skills. They had a couple of accounts payable positions available and would reach out to see if they could set up an interview.

That afternoon, we went for a drive with my aunt. There were a few old beach-bum-type apartments that were stinky and run-down, but they fit my budget and location preferences. That day, I snagged the phone number for one of the one-bedroom apartments and was to meet with the manager later in the week.

I drove around that week, going to a couple of interviews, knowing how much I needed to make to cover my rent and basic bills. I was offered two of the positions. I declined one because of some weird vibes I was getting from the to-be boss. It didn't feel right, and the things he was saying were warning signs. I reported those words back to the staffing agency, which was surprised, and had to get in touch with him to explain that it wasn't good behavior to say that to someone you're trying to hire, or in general.

Have you ever been in an interview when the environment around you looks ok, but something is screaming, "run"? Follow your intuition, it is there for a reason!

The other company I interviewed with was for a large food corporation, and I would be one of the few people handling accounts payable. Shortly after the interview, I found out they wanted me and offered me exactly what I needed to pay my bills and have a little left over. I was amazed and yet not surprised, as there was an internal knowing that it was all going to happen. However, for the first time, I was really grateful for the experience and knowledge that the "number-crunching desk job" and my mom had taught me years prior.

My New Apartment

That day, we met in what would now be my ground-floor single-bedroom beachy apartment. There was no view of the bay or beach, but I was still within walking distance. It had an old, dark tan carpet and one of those wall-mounted radiator heaters I hoped would provide enough heat in the winter without being a home to cockroaches. It was a small unit, but I didn't want any roommates. At this point, I didn't want any more girl drama; I just wanted to have fun and try living alone. Basically, I was ripping all the band-aids off at once as I created this new reality for myself.

There was a unit beside mine, and two on the second story; they all opened to the outside so that we could enter and exit our living rooms directly into the humid San Diego air. The four units I was now a part of were behind another four-unit building. The building I was going to be in backed up to the alleyway, as did my bedroom window, which was a new experience in itself. I left a bedroom that looked out to a gorgeous pasture where I could watch my horses graze on the green grass and went to this bedroom, where I kept my blinds closed so the homeless people couldn't see me changing into my jammies as they dug through the garbage right below my window. Clearly, I never opened that window either, as I am sure it wouldn't smell of potpourri and roses.

However, I felt safe—strangely, it may have had to do with the fact that all the units around mine had friendly, chill surfer men, and my aunt was just a few blocks away.

The end of the week came, and we moved all my stuff in, and yes, I furnished an apartment—except for my aunt and uncle, who gave me a black leather couch to borrow. I am a planner at heart and have been gathering items for the possibility of filling my own space. Like a deep call from my soul, I was preparing myself for who I was becoming. I had two sets of dishes and silverware. I thought I would need two because I grew up with my mom and heard funny stories about how she would often break dishes by accident, so I wanted to make sure I would have plenty.

My family helped me unpack everything, and I know it helped them get used to the idea of leaving me, although it was not easy for any of us.

Scott's Surprise

Scott also came down to help, and he spent an hour and a half scrubbing the tub and shower. I couldn't believe he would do that dirty job for me; I giggled in delight at how romantic I thought it was. So far, this relationship was one-eighty from anything I had ever experienced with a boyfriend, and I was delighted.

At the time, Scott worked nights on base as a mechanic for helicopters and a few hours during the day at another civilian aviation company to gain experience and get his A&P License, while also taking classes at Embry-Riddle for Professional Aeronautics. Again, who was this person? This man blew my socks off; he was so motivated. I hadn't ever been with someone like that. My previous boyfriend didn't go to college and barely knew how to type on a computer, even though he was two years older than I was. He had no ambition to plan for the future, let alone buy a house or save for retirement; he couldn't even get through one week without asking me for money to buy a hat to add to his two-hundred-hat collection. Remember, he had a full-time, good-paying job, but he blew it each week on mindless spending.

Scott, however, was getting four hours of sleep a night to make sure he was setting himself up for all of life's events.

Earlier in the week, my parents and I drove up to see him, which was 45 minutes north of where I would live. He met us at a Walgreens near where he had gotten off work at his second job. I happily climbed into his truck, and he asked my parents to follow him. Up to this point, he was living on base. However, he pulled up to a condo complex right outside the base and showed us a condo he had just bought—a beautiful, newly remodeled two-bedroom investment.

Again, who the eff is this guy? He was twenty-two years old and acted like a thirty-or forty-year-old. I was blown away, of course. I grew up around responsible parents, aunts, uncles, and a brother, but it really made me understand how far down the wrong path I went with that prior boyfriend. I didn't regret any of the lessons I learned, but my heart was profoundly grateful to finally be with a man of this caliber.

The interesting thing was that he saw me as that same caliber—a quality woman with her head on straight, ambitious, a sense of confidence, and grace. I lost my sense of self and couldn't see that part of me any longer. Stepping into his presence started to calibrate me back to who I was meant to be. He was like a mirror, reflecting to me all the things he knew me to be; he had seen them in me for years. However, looking at him now, I heard what he would say, which made me wonder whether it was true, but I still doubted myself. It seemed like a faint siren call back to myself in the dark depths of a storm I couldn't see through.

I was leery at the time that I somehow possessed those same qualities that made us a match, but not cautious enough to have my optimistic soul be brought down. I could feel what I desired in my heart starting to bloom again. I saw this new life as the door opened, and I got a glimpse of where I was being called to go. It was easy because the pull in that direction was strong and because I couldn't imagine staying the same, at the same place, doing the same job, surrounded by the same people.

It took God a while to get me to end the previous relationship; however, when He did, it was like years of catching up unfolded into this new reality. The woman I was meant to become and the life I was to build came flooding in because I dared to dream, I dared to leap, and in my mind, there was no other option. It was a no-brainer, no matter how terrifying it would be.

The Lesson

This was the first time I had been pushed to that degree outside of my comfort zone. It was the first time the people pleaser in me hadn't asked my parents or anyone around me whether they approved. I didn't do the typical grounding exercise of weighing the pros and cons.

I don't like weighing the pros and cons; I've done it most of my life, and you know where it got me? Confused. Back to where I started. On this decision, I felt the tug; I couldn't unsee the path. I hadn't thought about it and weighed it for months. I didn't ask whether I was qualified, ready, prepared, or capable. I just leapt, and all the pieces lined up.

I am a planner to the core, with a dash of love for taking risks. Now, instead of weighing the pros and cons, I check in with my intuition and body. In this case, I didn't think of all the things that could go wrong; I literally rode the coattails of the God-provided vibration, assuming all the things that could go right would. It was a quantum leap, a leap that would change everything in my life.

Reflection Questions

Sometimes, the most significant leaps we take define who we become. Look back at your own journey with these questions.

1. **When you look back, have you made a significant leap—a leap so big you had no option but to change and uplevel everything around you?** What was it?

2. **What is one decision in life you have made without the people pleaser asking for permission or getting stuck in the indecisive process?**

3. **Do you remember how you felt in those moments?** What patterns and habits changed because you spread your wings?

4. **Did you listen to doubt, especially that of others, or did you tune it out and hold the pose even when you were scared?**

5. **Is there a quantum leap calling to you right now that you've been resisting?** What would it look like to just go for it without weighing all the pros and cons for months?

CHAPTER 16
EXPANDING IN THE REBUILD

Have you ever gone on vacation somewhere and thought you would like to move to that location because you were more relaxed than you felt in years, only to realize when you moved there, the same problems followed you if you hadn't dealt with them? It is true: the only way that thing will change is if you change your internal reality.

Here I was, living in another state—city versus country—working in a massive corporation in a cubicle (you know how much I love that number-crunching desk job), and living on my own instead of with family. I had done it, changed everything about my outer world. However, being in this new relationship wasn't a magic wand that erased all the scars from my past or the damage from the previous relationship. I had struggles, worries that my new guy, who seemed to have his shit together, would pull the old crap that my last boyfriend had done to me. I needed to work on the internal part of this new life I was living.

Romantic Bliss and Steady Ground

Scott and I were having a blast; it felt like I was still on a romantic vacation. Every time we saw each other on the weekends, it was easy, fun, exhilarating, and divine to be together. It had been a few months since we started dating, and there was no drama, no questioning, and no doubt; he was steady and did what he said he would do. I felt the excitement pulsing between us every time we were together, and the desire and longing when we parted to face the responsibilities of our weekly work.

We were approached again in restaurants and stores by people who admired how we were showing up in the world and told us how much they enjoyed watching us interact. It happened so many times and made us laugh in surprise because we were so tuned into each other that the rest of the world blurred out.

He was healing so many wounds from my past just through our consistent interactions. Still, they were deep. I tried not to bring up my past and place any of the doubts on this new relationship; however, my love, the best time to do inner work is when you are being triggered. The only way I could really heal those scars was to be in a relationship with someone I deeply cared for. It is tough, it is raw, and as much as you don't want to place that burden on someone else, it is necessary in the process. He was healing those scars in me, and I was healing other relationship scars for him.

We didn't fight or argue; it was pure bliss. I remember thinking, "This is too good to be true; the other shoe will drop soon, I will find out he is a jerk, and then I will have to pick myself up and move on." That shoe never dropped; it wasn't going to, but my nervous system didn't know that.

His older sister had told him something back in high school that was brilliant in this situation. She told him dating is supposed to be fun and easy, and when I thought of that, I realized I was finally with the right person. It was all clicking, never in an insincere way but in a way that was so unbelievably natural and real, it just worked.

Many people will still marry the one who made them feel insecure, doubtful, and nervous because they thought that was the best they could do, and were afraid of rocking the boat and moving on. Relationships are not perfect; there are no perfect people. It does take work, and it can be the best, most robust, turned-on, supportive, and trustworthy thing in your life, but if the other person triggers you, do the work. If you break up with that person, don't try to do all the work before your next relationship with a counselor, waiting to get into a relationship with someone when you are done. Say yes now, and keep going to counseling, because that is when the triggers arise—when you are in a relationship with someone you care for, they will trigger all the wounds you need healed. Continue that relationship and counseling together until you can see those behaviors in yourself enough to change them for the better. If you stop going to counseling when you enter this new relationship, all those triggers will likely cause you to create the same problem in the new relationship.

Old Patterns Surfacing

Back to the story now. I was pushing myself outside of my comfort zone daily—keeping my bills in check, being responsible, and taking care of myself instead of always waiting on someone else. I was changing. It was as though I remembered a future when I would add value to the world and could do things; I was moving in terrified confidence. My safety was on edge living alone. The fear of not managing the small amounts of money I set as my cap was keeping me tight. Yet, every other piece of me was starting to expand.

I took time to realize how lost I had become in the previous relationship and friendships, and I gave myself empathy for the journey that had led to this point. I had a lot of time to reflect, as I wasn't a typical 22-year-old partying in the bustling party vibe town I was living in. I took my new life seriously and this new opportunity as a chance to expand—although I didn't view it in that way at the time, that is what I was doing.

I found myself being pulled back into old patterns of people-pleasing in my conversations at work and also trying to pay for multiple dinners and items in this new relationship, as I had in the previous one. There were times I wanted to pay even though I knew it would stretch me super tight on my next bill cycle, but that deep-down pain was pulsing hard through my body. A pain that if I am not giving in every possible way, I have no value. If I am not pleasing that other person and rising to their standards, they will not stay.

Scott was shocked by how many times I offered to pay, sometimes allowing it. I was a force to be reckoned with because I had built my house of cards as an insecure people-pleasing woman who showed her worth by being the worker and provider in a relationship. Yikes, that is pretty ick to say even now. My worth wasn't coming from a place of "I am worthy just because," or because he was attracted to the light inside of me, or even because I had value in who I was. In my mind at the time, a woman works endless hours, is at work even when she wants to be home, misses some of her kids' events, and then comes home to do many of the house's tasks and chores, seemingly being the breadwinner. That is what my mom showed me in her habits, and what my previous relationship had confirmed.

Don't get me wrong, my dad is a very stable, consistent, hard-working, and talented man, who showed me so much about patience. He was the one who could show up and drive me to most of my horse events because his job was more flexible than my mom's. The previous statement has less to do with how my dad showed up, but more about how energy is more impactful than words, and how a mom's words are essential, but how she treats and values or devalues herself will be the example her daughter will see or embody.

So there I was, with previous relational habits surfacing despite my change in scenery and move to a new environment—habits that were not welcome, challenging who I desired to be. Scott allowed me to pay here and there, and years later, he was mortified that he had even allowed it when I told him how tight my monthly finances were during that period of my life. I rebutted his shock with great pride in having risen and taken care of myself, realizing I could do hard things. It was a God moment, one that showed me what I was fully capable of. I genuinely believe it was the foundation of the new house I was building on a rock that wouldn't crumble when things got hard.

God was right to lead me to California.

I had moved there in January, and Scott proposed to me on the most romantic gondola ride in Newport Beach in May as the sun was setting, creating a glowing glisten on the water. I was so surprised—and yet not—because there was a deep knowing that this was the next step, that he was the one who matched my soul. It was a no-brainer. Again, I couldn't unsee a future with this Marine.

The Lesson

I knew I was led to shift my paradigm completely and start expanding into where I was meant to go. I knew it was God-led because I never asked others for permission, weighed their thoughts enough to persuade me, or questioned whether I could handle it. I never considered that I was barely making it as a sign that I shouldn't have made the move or that I should go back to how things were. I had faith in something I couldn't see, yet I could feel that, although things were nerve-wracking, my heart was being broken wide open to be rebuilt—rebuilt in my self-esteem and what I was capable of.

I learned I can do hard things and live to tell the story, all while rebuilding what I thought love and relationships should be. Although I would go on to be a people pleaser for many years, this was a rebuilding of the structure, my foundation—the beginning of releasing my inner stampede.

Calling In Your Match

They say when you meet the right person, they are meant to trigger the shit out of you to heal the wounds of your past, but that shouldn't happen in dating. Dating should be fun. I dare you to be open to the idea that it's expansive, exhilarating, and erotic. That you can be desired and lusted after. You, my love, need to set the stage and set your worth to call in your man.

You can't call him in if you never dream, if you never desire, and write down what you sincerely want in a spouse. If you are married now, write it down and say it daily as if you were married to that person. Feel it deeply in your soul and show up in ways he would reciprocate. That means act in a way that would attract the guy you desire.

Your guy may not do everything perfectly or the way you want. What if you shift? What if you start blowing his mind in a good way? What would his response be? As women, we can get so caught up in the "He's not doing it, why should I be the one to start?" Don't let yourself get stuck in the victimhood mentality, waiting on him to change. If you feel it, you are the one to start the shift; you are the lighthouse beaconing for a new outcome—he will thank you eventually.

Reflection Questions

It's time to get clear on what you want and who you need to become to call it in.

1. **Make that list—who is he, and who are you as his reciprocal?** A powerful, protective man isn't going to want a person who bitches and whines at him, telling him he isn't enough.

2. **How will you start rebuilding your relationship today?** Whether you're single and calling in your match, or married and reigniting the spark—what's one shift you can make toward what you desire in the relationship?

3. **What card will you remove from the house of cards you have created to shift into another reality?** What old pattern needs to go?

CHAPTER 17
IS THIS "BITCH" WORTH IT?

The proposal had happened, and now I was living in this insane reality. I was bursting with happiness I had never felt. I was going to get married, not to a man I had dated for years, and it was "just the next step," but because I had found someone who freaking chose me, and I him! I literally couldn't believe it—this insanely handsome and good man actually wanted me! He saw something in me that kept calling him back to the reality of pursuing me.

I have thanked God time after time that he placed that in Scott's heart, that Scott couldn't help but be drawn to me as though he had always known me, and we were meant to be together. I joke with him here and there about how I "married my stalker," but I didn't—and really, that isn't a funny joke—but he and I share a very odd sense of humor. He wasn't a stalker; he just knew, and I am so grateful that he did, because Scott was an answer to the rockets shooting from my heart that day in the mechanic shop with the old boyfriend, watching as a man oozed passion and love for his betrothed.

I yearned for that type of passion in a man, that type of love, that being seen, felt, heard, respected, and hungered for. Scott was the answered prayer from that moment, and that would have been enough, but then he came with a provider-protector body that I wouldn't recognize until years later. He made me feel so protected and held. It wasn't perfect—again, flawed humans trying to blend reality—but holy shit, it was 99% insanely hypnotic.

The Surprise Engagement Party

We were engaged now, and his family planned a surprise engagement party for us at their house one weekend. They arranged for my parents to come out and surprise us by opening the doors to their home. It was utterly shocking. I immediately started bawling, as I hadn't seen them in months and missed them dearly. It was a heartfelt gesture from my soon-to-be in-laws, and we will never forget the laughter we shared that weekend.

We were sitting around the table one evening at dinner when my soon-to-be mother-in-law asked me, "Rachel, when did you first know you loved my son?"

And I said, "Well, Sarah, this won't be our first wedding, so I think a piece of me has always known."

She was mystified. "WHAT? What do you mean, this isn't your first wedding?" she asked.

I paused for a moment, confused about why she was confused by this statement. I continued with the story that Scott and I got married in the fifth grade. She was baffled; laughter and delight erupted on the grand stairs and in the bedrooms on the second floor. She had no idea. Scott, a clever fifth-grader, knew things wouldn't go well at home with his dad if they got a call from the principal's office saying he was in trouble for kissing on the playground, so he intercepted the voicemail on the home's voice machine and deleted it. I am not sure why the school never tried to reach out again, but I do think God's hand was in it, sparing him from any further anger at home.

That night, we decided to send out invitations for our vow renewal, and we did.

The Looming Dark Cloud

The summer buzzed by with Scott and me dreaming about all the things we would love to have and do in the future as we walked hand in hand on the beaches of California. I imagined, of course, all the wedding dreams pouring out of my heart as I started to flirt with what I wanted this magical life moment to look like. There was a looming dark cloud far off in the distance, one we knew was approaching and was really hard to talk about, one that we didn't want to happen but knew was coming: Scott's second tour to Iraq.

He had enlisted just a couple of years after the September 11 attacks, and the troops were in full-fledged war deployment mode. This would be his second in only a year and a half; he knew what to expect, but he didn't know how he would now leave a girl he had loved since the second grade.

All the necessary steps were being taken. My apartment lease was month-to-month, so changing it was easy. He would need someone to live in his condo and take care of it while he was deployed for eight months. Given how California freeways work, I would need to get a different job, since I would be living on the north side, commuting in traffic, and what was now a 30-minute drive to my apartment would turn into an hour-and-a-half to his condo. It wasn't how I wanted to spend three hours of the day, so I decided to see what else I could find that was closer.

I went back to an agency that was amazing and got placed 20 minutes away, with a lovely drive along Highway 101, overlooking the ocean. My new boss was a dream and felt like a protector while Scott was away. He and his wife were so kind, and he steered me away from a few things he deemed unsafe. As he was a former Marine and cop, he knew the ins and outs of the hotspots around us. I will always be appreciative of him and his wife and the role they played in my life at that time.

The Phone Call

A few days before Scott deployed, we were in his kitchen, and my phone rang. I didn't know the number, but I answered anyway. I heard the voice, and my heart dropped. I felt the color drain out of my face, and I looked right at Scott as I froze. It was Zack.

I hadn't heard from him since I moved, and those interactions had been hard, as we were about to file a restraining order since he wasn't leaving me alone. He had started using drugs, something I couldn't fathom in my slightly goody-two-shoes heart, and honestly, I had a deep pit in my stomach, not knowing what he was capable of.

Scott immediately knew who it was and grabbed the phone. I witnessed his entire energy shift from the kind, supportive, funny, loving man I had been witnessing up until then to this strong, bold, rugged, fierce, commanding protector that emerged from his body. He proceeded to proclaim what Zack would and would not be doing from this point forward as though he were commanding an army of warriors.

Zack made up some dumb lie about being in touch with my family and that my family liked him, trying to steal any dignity back from this interaction with this fucking badass titan on the phone. It didn't work. Scott called out his bullshit, told him he wouldn't ever contact me again, outlined the consequences, and hung up.

I couldn't breathe. I was stunned and mind-blown, thinking again, who the fuck is this man? I leaped into his arms, and my heart gushed out not only a waterfall of thanks but deep sorrow for the people pleaser in me. The people pleaser was so unbelievably humiliated that he would have to handle something from my past relationship on this level. I felt so exposed and unveiled, like any moment he was going to think this "bitch" isn't worth it.

He didn't. He didn't move, like a freaking ox ready to withstand anything. He took it like a man. He called upon his deeply primal protector that day, and my heart swooned in a way I had never felt before. The drama from the old was dead; it tried to rear its head that day, but he crushed it like a freaking gladiator stepping on an ant on a sidewalk.

Saying Goodbye at the Tarmac

A few days later, we had to face one of the hardest things up until that point: his walking away on the tarmac at four in the morning to be flown to Iraq and placed in a war zone. Ever since I stepped foot into California, it felt like there was a plot twist after a plot twist, and my heart ached and grew weary with this one. I didn't grow weary with thoughts of leaving or of not supporting him; I grew tired of nervousness and the buildup of the unknown part of his safety.

It was the eeriest feeling I have ever felt, and if you have ever been part of saying goodbye to your loved one or even welcoming someone home from a war zone, you know it is a feeling that cannot easily be described or forgotten. It gets deeply embedded in your core memories and muscles, easily conjured up when you spend a few seconds thinking about that day. It was one of the hardest moments I have ever experienced. It is a time of pure faith, of stepping in daily to keep negative thoughts at bay, and of trusting that this is the plan.

I intentionally waited to do all my wedding planning while he was overseas so I would have something to keep my mind busy. We were to be married in July, just a couple of months after his return.

The Lesson

The approval-seeking, fixer, people-pleaser in me didn't want someone else to handle my battles; I didn't think he could handle them and still love me. If I were to be lovable, I needed to perform, not let my loose ends be shown and managed. Yet he didn't view it that way. The piece of the people pleaser that showed up that day was the controller—the do-it-all-myselfer.

But I couldn't do it myself. This guy needed a freaking ox to take him down, to see that I was being watched over and that he couldn't mess with me anymore. I felt so embarrassed and exposed and realized I had a tough time receiving from a man—receiving providership in the form of him paying for our dates, receiving protection in the form of standing up for me and not being bothered like I now owed him, and receiving love, a love that just stood, a love that saw the raw me and wasn't running for the door.

Reflection Questions

Learning to receive is one of the hardest lessons for a people pleaser. These questions will help you see where you're blocking love, protection, and support.

1.   **Where are you not allowing your partner, loved one, or husband to give to you?** Where do you struggle to receive, thinking you have to hold everything together? Do you judge other women for always receiving? If so, it might have you blocked from receiving because you are judging other women for that behavior.

2.   This can show up even in the silliest areas. You ask him to put away the dishes and then criticize him for doing it wrong. Be careful, my love, with the nuances you are sending him. **Where are you doing this?**

3.   **What would it feel like to let someone fight your battles?** To be protected without feeling like you owe them? Are you able to hold the pose and the discomfort, offering them a simple, loving thank-you, or would you need to make a larger gesture in return?

4.   **Are you performing to be lovable, or are you allowing yourself to be loved as you are—messy, exposed, and real?**

CHAPTER 18
TOO INSECURE TO ADVOCATE

After months of being separated, only able to speak twice a week, we were reunited and thrown into a wedding within less than two months of his setting foot back on US soil. It was a whirlwind of questions about the wedding, reuniting, and helping him adjust to having so many people around him after spending so long in the Iraqi desert.

We added to our soon-to-be family with a puppy, whom I named Petrie. She was rescued from a puppy mill, and I swear she called me to find her. She lived for fifteen years, and I wrote stories about her that are now published children's emotional support books. She was my first baby and had all the first experiences with us. I miss her dearly and know she is always with me.

We made the drive back to our home state to get married, three-month-old Petrie in tow. We decided to get married in the mountains of the small town where we grew up. It was a stunning location, set on a ski mountain, with a gorgeous lodge lined with windows overlooking an enchanting mountain range. It was July, and the weather was beautiful.

The Wedding Day

The day came, and I felt a deep sense of peace radiating through my body. My friend from an earlier chapter, whom I backed out of being maid of honor, was at my wedding. Again, I was impressed by her grace at that moment; she commented that day that I was so calm and peaceful, which baffled her. I thought it was strange that she thought it was weird. I just told her, "What is there to stress about? I get to marry my best friend."

I think when you are genuinely meant to be together, it doesn't matter what goes wrong at the wedding—the day you have been planning for months—the only thing you care about is saying your I do's and celebrating with your friends and family.

Little things did go awry that day. My two male cousins, whom I asked to show up and help direct cars where to park, showed up wearing Daisy Dukes, ridiculous shirts, funny cowboy hats, and boots—a sight that had a lot of people confused as they pulled in, I am sure, questioning who they were and what type of wedding this would be. I should have known better, asking them to do something serious when they are humorous individuals, yet I didn't care, and now it adds to the event's charm.

We were to be married right outside the lodge on a grassy cliff overlooking an insanely gorgeous view, yet God had other plans; it rained and rained and rained. I didn't even miss a beat. "Let's move it inside." It would be more cramped, but only during the ceremony, then we would head upstairs to the open room where the reception was being held.

My wedding was on point with my black-and-white decorating soul. It was black and white with red roses, and I loved it. The rain added a romantic, cozy vibe, and candles were lit along the large windows facing the mountains. We held it later in the day, so it became this softly lit, romantic haven that felt like God himself was smiling down upon our union. It was magical, and I wouldn't change a thing.

Except my hair.

The Hair

I had grown it down almost to my waist so I could have cascading curls, slightly lifted and falling down my back. I communicated that to the stylist, but I wasn't clear. I sat in the chair earlier that day and watched her do something to my hair that I didn't want. Guess what, the people pleaser in me was having a rage party and wasn't going to be interrupted and told to get the heck out. Nope, it continued its party of one, and I continued to sit in silence, not wanting to hurt the hairdresser's feelings that it wasn't what I wanted.

I regret that deeply. I don't care about the other things going differently at the wedding, but there I was again, sitting to get my hair done on one of the most cherished days of my life, and I couldn't let her know this wasn't my vision. The people pleaser still ran deep.

The Reception and Beyond

It was a lovely evening filled with laughter and dancing, ending at McDonald's at midnight because that was the only thing open in this tiny town. We were both starving because we had been too busy to eat much. I remember sitting in the passenger seat in his truck like a poofy cotton ball. I couldn't even see out the dashboard, and the server in the drive-through line was surprised to see a bride and groom. We didn't care; we were just hungry and so ecstatic that we were married.

The Honeymoon

We jetted off on a honeymoon my now-husband paid for. We had talked a few months prior about combining our resources, and I came clean about having a small savings account. It had been much larger; however, it was swept away, little by little, because I said yes when I really wanted to say no to my previous relationship. He handled it greatly and knew I was a responsible, reliable person, and this didn't bother him.

Yet again, I writhed with insecurity as I admitted to a man how deeply flawed my finances were. Not because I had debt—I only had a tiny amount left on a car loan and nothing else. He looked at me with empathy and confusion, wondering why I thought he would find this so despairing for our relationship. The way I viewed it at the time was not as "wow, I come with barely a hint of debt," but instead "wow, I come with no large savings and am not worthy of adding to our now joined bank account."

As I write this, I can feel how uncomfortable I was in this conversation, and tears well up as I think about how I believed my worth as a woman was measured by how much I could provide financially and through my work ethic. This wouldn't be until I became a mother that its ugly head would turn into a three-headed dragon, and I would be fighting said three-headed dragon like a tiny mouse with a toothpick.

Anyway, we headed to our magical honeymoon in Mexico, where I ate salads without even thinking the lettuce had been washed in the same water I was avoiding to avoid Montezuma's revenge. Well, this proper girl was exposed to her IBS issues. What a joy I was, I'm sure. We still had a wonderful time despite those moments of an upset stomach. We enjoyed long, moonlit, hot, and sweaty nights and long talking walks on the beach. We had a couple of massages next to each other on the ocean, and my husband claims he got "extra", with the lady masseuse's long arm hair tangling with his leg hair. He hasn't preferred massages from anyone other than me after that experience.

We arrived home from our honeymoon and were quickly thrown into the reality of life together. We had a misunderstanding that led to our first fight, and it quickly showed me how communication alone can make or break an intention. We resolved it quickly, but we will never forget our first fight the day after our honeymoon.

The Lesson

There are so many lessons from this moment in my life, but the one I want to point out, although it seems petty and insubstantial, is not speaking up for changing my hair. The lesson isn't about my hair; the hair was just the issue. The problem was that the self-sacrificing people pleaser in me still didn't have the tools to communicate and advocate for myself on the biggest day of my life, when what the bride wants should matter. When I look at our wedding photos, I see, number one, an insanely romantic wedding, and, number two, a girl who still didn't know how to speak up for fear of hurting someone else. She was willing to have something she didn't like on one of the best days of her life to spare someone else's feelings.

It seems small, but if you are a people pleaser, you know that it is just another struggle for the battle that lies within.

Reflection Questions

In certain circumstances, self-sacrifice is an excellent quality, but that wasn't what this was. It was my choice, my day. I was the only one who could make this choice, and my house of cards was trembling as I thought of speaking up at that moment.

1. **Think about a recent moment when you stayed silent about what you wanted. What stopped you from speaking up?** What did you fear would happen?

2. **If you could go back to that moment, what would you say differently?** Practice writing it out or saying it aloud. Imagine the next time you could be hit with something similar, and play out how you would handle it.

3. **Where in your life right now do you need to advocate for yourself—even in the "small" things?** Remember: if it matters to you, it's not small.

CHAPTER 19
EDITING YOURSELF

We now lived in lovey-dovey fairytale land, knowing Scott had to finish his stint in the Marine Corps and that a third deployment was on the horizon again—a thing he had to tell me while he was on his second deployment and on my actual bridal shower day. He didn't intend it to happen that way. Still, he had to choose whether we would get married and he would leave two months after, or if he would extend his contract a few more months and not have to deploy until spring, giving us at least six months to spend together as newlyweds. We had to make that choice right then.

We chose the latter, therefore getting to at least spend our first major holidays as a newlywed couple together. We faced another deployment—my second with him and his third in five years—it was pretty intense. We decided, despite his ability to cruise through the ranks and work his way up quickly, not to re-up in the military, and he would be honorably discharged shortly after his return from the third tour.

He was about to finish his degree in Professional Aeronautics. He was still accruing hours toward his A&P. We knew we couldn't keep doing these tours at the rate he was going, as they put all the security we had built on the line, and we didn't want to start a family with a tour always looming around the corner. His third tour was a success, and he thankfully returned home safely, receiving a couple of medals for honorable tasks he had performed while deployed. I will never forget the day he got off the white buses on the base, and I knew he was home safe, never to return to the war zone again.

Moving to Oregon

In the meantime, we were discussing where we wanted to move when he was released. It was like throwing a dart at a dartboard as we jumped all around the US and even contemplated moving abroad. We didn't want to stay in California, yet we didn't want to go back to our home state. I sincerely wanted to explore more of what was out there and have another adventure.

We spoke of Oregon. I flew there with my mom to check it out while he was in Iraq, and I fell in love with it. I brought back all I had discovered, and he agreed, still, while on tour, to move to a place he had never visited. He isn't picky; that is apparently my job in our relationship.

He returned home, and all of our belongings were in a "box" truck he had decided we would buy before he left. It wasn't one that most people would go for; looking at it made your eyebrows raise. Some even thought it would be an excellent canvas for graffiti, so they decided to add their own art one night while it was parked at our condo. It had its own personality, and sometimes it was questionable whether it would make it to the following location. Scott reassured me, and I agreed to buy it, knowing the man was deeply mechanically inclined and had rebuilt many cars growing up.

The day came that we drove off the Marine Corps base for the last time. He would now be in the reserves, not on active duty, and it felt like a foreign land to walk into. It was freeing yet confusing and exposing; however, he had set himself up correctly by spending his time well in school. I was just happy to have my man back safe and sound, and another unknown journey ahead of us.

Somehow, I led, inspired, or was part of moving to another state without jobs or a place to live. My parents liked to humor us by helping us move. I am sure they wanted to witness how this ridiculously faithful journey would turn out yet again. They were so awesome in helping us drive states away again with our caravan—my 4Runner, Scott's truck, and this giant rolling box truck filled with our entire life's belongings. Petrie was always up for a road trip, and I propped her up on a box with her bed on top, as she loved seeing where she was headed.

We coasted into Portland, milking the last bit of the transmission in the box truck. We parked it at a hotel on the other side of the busy freeways, and I am sure my father was thinking not-so-nice thoughts about who chose the hotel we would be staying at, since we had to cross multiple freeways to get there, and the truck was having issues. He and Scott had taken turns driving this thing, and it was barely holding together. The transmission was starting to fail, and apparently, a hole in the floor blew in during the early January weather, leaving them shaking upon arrival. A hot shower that night was well received, and my parents truly deserve rewards for all the moving shenanigans they participated in with us.

The next day, we went house hunting. We decided to rent a tiny little house at the end of a cul-de-sac, in a neighborhood in Vancouver, Washington, right across the gorge bordering Portland, Oregon. I wanted to be downtown Portland in an old house with character, but Scott wanted something more accessible; he was right—it was a better call. We rented out our condo in California during this time and now have a small house with a large backyard for Petrie. I could use my cosmetology degree in Oregon, just ten minutes away, and he could finish his Bachelor's degree, as Portland has an Embry-Riddle campus near where we lived.

Scott got a job at an auto parts store, where he had worked before joining the Marine Corps. He wasn't thrilled about this idea but knew he needed to take it, as it would work well with his school hours. I found a job at a salon in Portland, and we settled into living on our own, away from anything we had ever known. It was one of the best things we ever did as newlyweds, reconnecting after so much time apart due to deployments.

The Dinner Party Incident

During these first moments together, we had gone to visit some friends at their house for dinner, whom we were getting to know. We had them over first for dinner, and we enjoyed lots of laughing and stories over a manicotti dish I served. A month or two later, they invited us over for dinner, and when I offered to bring something, she suggested dessert. Ok, I was on it. I love making this delicious brownie, pudding, and Cool Whip trifle displayed beautifully in a trifle dish and sprinkled with fresh berries. I took it as my dessert.

We had a lovely evening, and then, as we were leaving, the people-pleaser party started. She complimented me on my dessert and dish, so I gave her my dish. I told her it was for her and that I wanted to bring her something that wasn't a "usual bottle of wine." When it came out of my mouth, I nearly fell over in disbelief at myself. Did I seriously say that? Number one, wine is fantastic, especially when it is gifted to you, which she did a month prior at my house. I literally just insulted the gift she brought us. I was so busy trying to say and do all the right things that I put my damn foot in my mouth. I said it during all the hugs and goodbyes, and I was so shocked that I didn't know how to correct it at the time.

We got in the car and started the hour-long drive home. I felt horrible—so rude and so ungrateful—but that wasn't my intention. On the drive home, I was cycling through what a terrible person I was and the shame of saying something so rude. My new husband didn't know how to help, except to say, "It wasn't a big deal." He didn't know what was happening and definitely didn't understand why I was so triggered.

The Shame Loop

I looped it around in my head repeatedly, not because I wanted to stay in a state of suffering, but because of my people-pleasing perfection: "don't hurt anyone," "say nice things to everyone," "watch my tone," echoed in my heart and mind. I couldn't stand it, so I called her. She answered the phone, and I profusely apologized for my rudeness. She accepted it but shrugged it off, affirming she didn't care, and now she had a fabulous new gift. As much as I appreciated her kindness, I still couldn't stop the shame I felt.

"Hi, it's me again, Rachel, people-pleasing over-giving extraordinariness." Who knows how to make things bigger than they actually were. That memory literally stayed with me for a couple of years. It raised its ugly head, reminding me what a bitch move that was for a couple of months right after, then it slowly quieted. We didn't see them in person again because they moved back to their home state to raise their children near family; however, when I thought of that person, an insane wave of guilt would wash over me. Even though it had been months or even a year, I would feel like all my insides were wide open again, with all my flaws hanging out. But they weren't. She honestly didn't care, but I had a deep wound that was eating away at me. A wound of not saying the perfect thing, of hurting someone else's feelings, even though it was unintentional.

The Lesson

There had been other instances before this, many of them while I was growing up, when I was told I had a tone or that the way I positioned my reply could be taken as rude or hurtful to the other person. Listen, yes, we all need to learn what is appropriate and inappropriate language. We can't just walk around spouting things out all the time; it's not kind or well-received. However, I came here with a kind heart. I didn't like to see anyone hurt, especially by my words or actions. I didn't need as much fine-tuning as I received as a young adult. This created the "good little girl" people pleaser.

The Micro-Management

It went from a few nips and tucks, which would've been enough, to the feeling I was being perfected. It caused me to hold so much in and create a whirlwind of looping thoughts and anxiety in my brain. I tried so hard to say things just right, but the problem was that if I even slightly messed up my tone, I felt enormous shame and guilt about what I said. My mom, "the nip and tucker," is a vibrant, fun-loving, deeply caring person with a massive heart for being the first to offer help, just like her mother did; however, within that deep caring came the molding of me and the critiquing of what I said. It wasn't because she was mean or a bad person; it's actually because she deeply desired to treat others with respect. Within that, however, it taught me to edit myself constantly.

The Persistent Loop

I learned that day that when I am not peaceful and genuine, it all bottles up inside of me, and a random outburst of freedom barrels out of my mouth. Bottling it up is one side of the coin; the other is the persistent looping that seems to plague you for days, weeks, months, and even years after you say something. Each time the memory comes up, shame accompanies it.

Reflection Questions

1. **What, my dear, are you carrying?** What have you been dragging behind you like a sack of shit that weighs fifty pounds?

2. **What is it that you are ready to free yourself from because the other person most likely doesn't even care or remember?**

3. **Where are you ready to stop carrying shame around something you never intended to hurt anyone with?** It may be something that you can see as a protection mechanism for you.

4. **Where are you editing what you really want to say?** What would it feel like to just be genuine instead of perfect? What would you say if you knew that you would be safe, loved, and seen?

CHAPTER 20
A NEW PATH

Settling In

We were in a full-fledged playhouse zone; it felt like a dream come true for the little girl inside me who had longed for a husband someday. We had found friends at a local church we had been going to. I had been curiously finding out how I could have a different relationship with God in a Baptist church, versus my experience of Catholicism, which I experienced growing up. I was baptized Catholic at a young age, and we went to services on Christmas and Easter, and sometimes in between. We were not devout Catholics in the way most were led to serve and show up; however, I do appreciate that a church and God were introduced to me as a child.

Being in a Baptist church felt like a party in comparison to the Catholic traditions and rituals. I really started to form a relationship with God, Source, and a higher power. It's as though it clicked, and I finally understood that I could have a personal relationship with God. The sermons were so understandable and relatable that I couldn't help but desire a deeper connection with the divine. I personally believe I wasn't meant to be a Catholic or be labeled toward any religious group. As the years went on, I would form my own relationship with God, the Universe,

Source, and Higher Power. I am grateful for the understanding, and I deeply respect most religions amongst us. Our time at this Vancouver church really opened the door to experiencing God in other ways, and it made me start thinking back to those experiences from my childhood, when I thought I saw angels. We had built a community of friends from this church, and it felt like we were finally settling in after a lot of instability with the tours; it felt sincerely welcomed.

I was working at a hip little salon in north Portland, enjoying being back behind a chair, helping people feel good about their hair, while Scott was sacrificing his desire to never work at this auto shop again, knowing he needed a job. He humbled himself as any good man would to bring in money while we were on our adventure and while he was finishing his degree—a quality I admire so much. He would work during the day, take a few night classes in Portland, then arrive home at ten or later, making it a very long day for him.

Life with Petrie

Petrie and I would be fully submerged in bed under a tundra of covers to stay warm. The house we were staying in was a small, one-level, three-bedroom house with cold, laminated floors throughout. I didn't know how much it would cost to keep the furnace running in the winter, so I carried around a portable heater wherever Petrie and I would be in the evenings after I got home from work. I could've tried testing the heater, but at the time, in our minds, we were trying to keep the bills down, as we had both taken a pay cut. We had a nice savings and were trying to keep building it—who needed heat anyway on those damp, rainy, cold winter days? He always laughed when he came into our room, and I was asleep, looking like I was in Alaska, curled up like an Eskimo, barely to be found beneath the pile.

The home had a pretty large backyard, especially after living in an apartment and condo for the previous years. Petrie was Queen of her backyard and tried daily to convince the squirrels that they weren't allowed to run on top of her fence. It never fully worked, but she was relentless in not ceasing her mission. There was a nice glass sliding door in the kitchen that opened to the grassy backyard. The sun would shine in and kiss the countertops, giving the whole space a warm glow as we woke up. I would let Petrie out that door to go potty. When she was ready to come back in, she would stand, staring at me, licking the glass as I cooked whatever I was making in the kitchen. Her little black eyes were like marbles that could see right through your flesh into your soul. She was intense in the best way. She was soft, kind, and welcoming to all. She was feisty when she felt the job arise. She was my companion when Scott was busy, and she always wanted to do and be whatever and wherever I was. She would actually sniff my clothes when I dressed in the morning, I assume, in her attempt to see what type of adventure she would get to partake in that day. If I had my hangout jeans on, she would get pumped, as she knew it might be a dog park or a walk-down-the-street kind of day.

The Dirt Bikes

One outing she couldn't partake in was our dirt bike rides through the surrounding trails of what felt like a magical rainforest. I had never had a dirt bike. I was willing to try balancing a motorcycle only on somewhat soft dirt trails, not on paved streets. Scott and I found two matching Yamahas—his, of course, was a supercharged 450, which was a beast, and mine was a little 125 to putt around on. I, of course, took my time figuring it out and trying to get braver about going faster. However, I still giggle at the image of myself—I sat with my back straight, tooting around on it like I was Nanny McPhee or a circus clown.

This motorcycle had a clutch system that you had to get the right feel for to move forward without stalling the engine and killing the motor. I had gotten pretty good at it since the first vehicle I drove was a standard with a clutch, and that is all I knew until my most recent automatic 4Runner. It was fun; we tooted along easy-to-medium trails for me. Scott was better and could've gone on the rugged trails, but you are only as good as your weakest link, and that was me.

The Wheelie

We were starting one day on a slight incline. I didn't want to kill the bike, so I gave it a bit of extra juice. Before I knew it, the front tire was off the ground. I was riding a wheelie on a two-tire motorbike. I rode it for probably 30 feet and realized I needed to let go of the throttle to set it down. I quickly released my grip on the throttle, and the front tire hit the ground. I put my feet on both sides of the bike as I pulled in the brake and turned around to look back at my husband, who sat there, jaw dropped. I just unintentionally popped a wheelie, rode it out, and balanced myself down without even trying. I screamed in delight, and we both started laughing.

The Challenging Trail

I was getting a little more confidence, and we decided to try another "medium" level trail we hadn't been on. The trails were stunning; the only dirt you could see was the actual path you rode on, about a foot wide. Evergreens lined the trail, reaching high into the sky toward the sun, casting shadows over the ground cover, which was living its best life in the perfect environment, thriving wildly, out of control. It was gorgeous and an absolute delight to ride or hike anywhere. The ferns and moss growing up the trees made me feel like I was in a tropical rainforest somewhere in South America, or the thought kept occurring to me that maybe someone from the Twilight series would pop out behind a tree around the next corner.

We started down this new trail, and I was doing my usual straight-back Nanny McPhee/clown look as I meandered through the trees. There were a few spots that got rocky and slightly questionable, but I hoped those were behind me, and smooth sailing would continue. Still, I was wrong; it just kept getting worse, as if it were gently inviting me to a challenge I didn't want to accept. Scott was ahead of me at least forty feet, and the sound of the dirt bikes echoed through the trees. We were out in the boonies, and we had been down this trail for at least 45 minutes now. Surely it would end soon, so I kept pushing forward. He couldn't hear me, even if I chose to stop and decide to turn around. So I kept going, white-knuckling my way through the rocky hills that were coming at me.

Facing the Giant

He finally stopped up ahead, and my heart was so glad until I realized what he stopped at the base of. It was a steep, jagged hill filled with boulders and sharp, pointy rocks to get around. There was little room to weasel our tires through at speed, trying not to run into the boulders while avoiding killing the engine on this vertical, long incline. My heart raced. How was I going to do this? This was too much. I am not that skilled, and I don't want to get injured!

He looked at me and asked, "What do you think?"

I wanted to scream and curl up into my Eskimo blankets on my bed at home. My mind flashed to being anywhere but here right now. I felt as though all the nerves under my skin were lit up in fight mode, saying go anywhere but there.

"I don't know if I can do that," I replied with trembling, staring in my hands.

He got out the map and looked at our location. "I think this is the last part of it. I think the main road is just past the crest of this hill, and we will be done," he said, looking at me as if he were trying to read my face.

Oh my gosh, I was done. I wanted to get off the bike, get in the truck, and leave. My nervous system didn't like either option. I could turn around and take the path I already knew. This path will now take at least an hour to get back to the truck, and it's starting to drizzle again and get darker, or I can face this beast and try not to injure myself. I repeated out loud what I was thinking and asked again whether he really felt the main dirt road was just beyond this hill, and he confirmed, yes.

He also offered one more option. "I can ride my bike up there, park it, walk back down, and ride yours up too," he stated.

Oh, my mind said yes! Take that option; let him figure it out. He is a better rider; it'll be no big deal for him. I was about to take that option, dreaming of the heater in the truck and warming up after a cool afternoon ride, when my heart spoke as if it were a human looking at me in my own eyeballs, making me face something it knew I was capable of.

"Rachel, you can do this, you can do hard things. How will you feel if you don't try?"

My head countered with "This is dumb, are you willing to get hurt and risk injury so that you can prove you can do hard things?"

Oh my gosh, I was in a battle within myself. Scott had given me options. I could take two options that were the easy way out, or the path back that I already knew and expected. I looked again at this giant, breathed deeply into my belly, and somehow the words "I will do it" came out of my mouth. I wanted to retract immediately, but I couldn't. My heart wouldn't let me; it knew I needed to face this fear to grow as a rider. I couldn't just stay on the easy path my whole life—I mean, I could—, but I knew something deep down would get bored, and the people pleaser would feel so guilty in keeping Scott on the easy path with me.

The Climb

As all these thoughts were still looping in my head, I watched him man-handle his beast and make it to the top. It was hard, but he made it seem effortless. He parked his bike, got off, and started walking down the trail, offering again to ride mine. I shouted now, since he was far away, "I've got it."

I popped my butt on the seat, put on my helmet, said a little prayer, and hit the throttle. I kept a good pace and knew that the last thing I wanted to do was kill the bike and let it roll backwards down the hill, so like a bull coming out of its pen angry at the world, I gave it plenty of gas. There's no way I was going to let this take me down. I maneuvered on and off with the throttle and decided where to place my tire next. I could only look a few feet ahead and use logic to determine the next move. I just knew I couldn't stop. If I stopped, that is when the trouble would happen. I felt jostled around on the seat with the back tire being pushed left and right between the big rocks, making it hard for my butt to stay on the seat. Yet, the hill was too steep for me to stand and keep my balance.

I remember I was a few feet from the top, and tears started to leak from my eyes. The feeling of my butt staying on the seat and reattaching to the bike began to happen, and suddenly I was on flat ground with the road to the truck about 50 feet in front of me. I slammed on the brake, kicked the kickstand to the ground, turned off the bike, jumped off, fell to my knees, and literally kissed the ground beneath me.

My husband was laughing and sending me all the whoops and hollers, affirming that I just made that hill my bitch. But I think of it more as Mother Earth and God gently held me up all the way, so I wanted to give them some heartfelt love and recognition. We rode back down the hill to escape the rain that had started quickly, loaded up, went home, took a hot shower, and fell asleep on the couch from the adrenaline crash once I knew I was safe, warm, and comfortable.

The Lesson

I learned that day that to grow, to become something you are striving to be or do differently, you can't take the same path you have been on to get there. You can have help along the way, but you also won't grow if others do the hard stuff for you. I had to face the giant before me. I knew deep down that was the only way to grow, expand, and become the type of rider I desired to be.

In life, if you want to change, you have to take another path, my dear. Sometimes that path is scary, and you feel as though you are facing a giant three-headed dragon as a mouse again, fighting with a toothpick. You will be amazed to learn what you can do. "I don't know where to begin, and I cannot accomplish that"—when you hear that voice, see that it is there to keep you safe. It is the part of the brain whose sole job is to ensure you survive. It doesn't mean that it is an actual life-threatening danger. It means you might actually blow through the glass ceilings you have placed above your head and into the next level of your desires.

As a people pleaser, you will have glass ceilings in most areas of your life. I learned that if you start stepping into discomfort in one of those areas and accomplish it—it will light the path for the next breakthrough.

Reflection Questions

You cannot reach a new destination by staying on the same path. These questions will help you identify where you're playing it safe and where you need to choose the scarier path.

1. **Where, my dear, are you continuing to stay on the same path, yet sincerely hoping for a different destination?**

2. **What areas in your life are you too afraid to step off the path you are on and convinced you don't have what it takes?**

3. **Do you think perhaps that the scary path—the one you're avoiding—is the exact path that will actually lead to the destination you have been dreaming of for all this time?** What doors would open if you walked down that path?

4. **What "giant hill" are you facing right now?** What would it feel like to say "I've got it" and just go for it?

CHAPTER 21
CLOAK OF IDENTITY

Life in the Pacific Northwest

Scott and I lived in the Pacific Northwest for about two years. We had a lot of adventures in the woods and on the hour-and-a-half drive to the stunning coastline, a coastline I have always thought of as having a spiritual presence for me, even now. I confirmed it again on a recent trip to Cannon Beach. Our nephew was getting married in Portland, and we thought it would be a great idea to show our daughter where we spent the first years of our marriage, taking a little time before the wedding. She was quickly mesmerized by the stunning cliffs and fog that rolled in over the sand. It was delightful to see her connect with the seagulls and be enchanted by a cliff line I can't help but feel impacted by. There are everlasting memories from this short period that were so impactful on our marriage. With so much time spent apart in our relationship due to tours to Iraq, we felt disconnected at times, wondering how to reconnect with the power we knew our relationship had. Our time in Vancouver was the adventure that plugged us back in and bumped us back into our voltage zone.

If you have ever experienced a spouse going off on a military tour, especially in an active war zone, you know how things feel when you merge your lives back together. My hat goes off to people who have children while experiencing those changes. I respect all the men and women who volunteer to serve in the armed forces; it's not a job—it's a way of life that many take great pride in, and they are held to a rigorous set of rules and regulations that govern what they can and cannot do. I will always have respect for those men, women, and their families, not to mention a deep admiration for the man I married and the way he chose to serve his country, and always strives to be the best at his position.

Missing the Sun

We were missing family after some time in Vancouver and starting to realize that the sun's hibernation in the winter wasn't for us. We grew up in a mountain town where it would snow for a day or two, then the sun would come out, and a million little diamonds would reflect off the snow, lighting up the outdoors even more. I love the rain, the way it thunders, lightning, and the smell as it hits the mountain air. The rain of the Pacific Northwest was different. It was relentless, and mainly a drizzle that made it wet to do anything. Moss was growing on our sidewalk, and little snails were enjoying living their best life on the way up to our front door. It was gorgeous, but after some time there, what we craved most was the sun.

We knew we wouldn't settle there; it was too far from any family, and we knew that someday, if we wanted to have kids, we would like them to be within a shorter, drivable distance from our hometown.

The Whisper of What's Next

I was also bored. I had poured my heart into cosmetology and had success in Portland, but I kept hearing a whisper to my soul: Is there something else? Cosmetology—is a science, and you get to create a space for making people feel their best. It's a super fun career, and I loved it; there is so much to the angles of cutting and the science behind color mixture. I should've been content. However, I couldn't shake the call upon my heart that I'm ready for what's next.

Scott and I are both impatiently patient people; we will wait, but when we move, we move swiftly. Scott is a powerhouse, living what felt like what most people accomplish in a lifetime; he was finishing in four years, and I was no longer satisfied with the art I was practicing as a cosmetologist. I wanted something else, but then the voice crept in, "Rachel, you are not smart enough." It would come and go as I pondered what I desired to do. I am an incredibly patient person, yet when it comes to a deep gut-opening inclination, I move, and I move fast.

Finding a New Path

I couldn't shake it, so I started looking into shorter school options, as I didn't want to spend the next four years getting a bachelor's degree. It just wasn't my calling. I used my time off each weekend to research the type of careers that would be an asset to us, while Scott was finishing his last classes. I shadowed a physical therapist to see if I wanted to become a physical therapy assistant, and although it was cool, it didn't quite hit the mark. However, I knew I felt called to the health industry, but didn't want to commit to nursing or hospitals, where I would be administering medications; it just didn't align with my core values. I am so grateful for the men and women who offer their support on a hard day in someone's life and recognize that duty wasn't for me.

I finally came across the Medical Assistant and Phlebotomist roles. I was intrigued; it was a less-than-a-year-long, everyday, intense submersion program. I would be able to work in clinics rather than hospitals, and even pursue skin care, which would be a great pairing with my cosmetology license. I let it sit for a day, talked with Scott, and found out that the training institution had a location in our home state, which would help us get closer to family and settle down a bit. I called the school in that city, obtained information about the program, spoke with my husband, and enrolled in the following program, which starts in just a few months.

Another Move

There we were again, moving. It seemed to happen a lot in this relationship, but there was always an adventure ahead that terrified and excited me, and an ascension I didn't realize would come with each move. Scott was able to get another job at the auto repair chain located in this new city. This time, I did some preparation and found an apartment in one of the suburbs near his new work location. There was also a lot of aviation near where we chose our apartment, so we thought that would be helpful as he started applying for civilian jobs with his new degree.

We had time while we were in Vancouver to work on the old box truck and get it in better shape, as it would have barely limped on its next stint of our journey and most likely left us stranded on the side of the road. During our adventures in Vancouver, we had time to snag an old CJ7 jeep that I helped my husband work on in our garage. We used that box truck and some ratchets to lift the entire jeep frame off its undercarriage, leaving only the chassis for him to work on as he desired. Life with Scott has been eyebrow-raising in many moments. I guess God knew we would work well together, accepting each other's passions and dreams, even if we didn't understand what the heck the other one was doing.

My ever-supportive and giving parents flew out and helped us again drive our two vehicles and box truck back to our home state. Of course, they were buzzing the whole time, thrilled that it would be a little over a half-day drive to where they lived and that it would now be so much easier to see us. We settled into another small apartment, unable to unpack everything. We left many things in the box truck and parked it at my parents' house for the time being. Scott started work, and I attended my first day of school for orientation.

Facing My Insecurities

I sat in a conference room, nerves bursting under my shirt. I had just been inspired to move to a school I didn't think I was smart enough to attend. I was an average-to-below-average student in high school; my friends were "smarter" than I was because they mostly got straight A's. I wasn't taught how to study well, and, let's be honest, I didn't like studying. I didn't enjoy school other than the social aspect, and I just wanted to ride my horse and be with that previous confidence-stealing boyfriend. I wasn't smart; I knew it because I had proof. I was the dumbest one in my group of friends, according to my school grades, and because I never pushed myself—I let it define me and accepted that I wasn't the "smart" type. My inner story had become "awe, I'm just not that smart to go to college."

There I sat, in a room with 18-20-year-olds who had mainly just gotten out of high school and were in the habit of studying. I was 26. I felt like an old crow amongst the people in the room, as though they were going to see right through me and call me out that I was dumb and not smart enough to be here. I sat in my discomfort and hung on every word the director said about what to expect over the next year. There was a section toward the end in which they spoke of the "Director's Award," which is essentially the Dean's award at a college or university. My ears perked. I couldn't imagine keeping my grades high enough and maintaining perfect attendance to achieve this award. Still, something deep inside, underneath all the layers of doubt and insecurity, caught a glimpse of a desire that it was mine.

Setting My Own Standard

I went home after a quick stop at the store to get supplies for our first assignment, which, looking back, was funny: they wanted us to create a poster board about ourselves and present it on our first day of class, which was tomorrow. I sat in the little living room doing arts and crafts on my poster board, decorating it after I filled it with information. I was done, the room was a mess, and I showed Scott. "Do you think this will work?" I asked, genuinely concerned that it wouldn't be good enough.

He looked at the poster board and looked at me a few times, trying to gauge if I was serious. "Babe, this is over the top, yeah, it's enough," he replied with amazement. He continued, "Most people are going to write on it with a Sharpie and call it good." He knew because he wouldn't have put that much effort into a poster board during his school days.

"Ok," I said. I would trust him. I showed up the next day and was definitely the only one who went to that great an extent on a poster board, which set my pace. It set my tone, not in a way of "having" to uphold that, but in a way that my mind confidently determined my new standard.

Proving Myself Wrong

The first six weeks of accelerated classes were taught by a single teacher and covered anatomy and physiology, among other introductory topics. She would then allow us to move on to the next teacher, who we would spend the rest of the time in her class learning all we needed to know to become medical assistants and phlebotomists. As our time in the first class ended and we journeyed to the second phase of the program, the original teacher approached me and asked if I would speak to the next group to inspire them to believe they could do this and overcome their nerves.

You see, I didn't just go to class and pass some tests and homework; I aced them. I showed up on time—which is early in my mind—listened to every word carefully, and went home and studied. I was dedicated, and it showed. I wasn't just passing; I was leaving with an end grade of 100% in the class—not just the tests, not just the homework—but that is how I ended the classes. This blew me away! I went in and gave a quick 5-10-minute speech about how I hadn't thought I was capable, but that if they put in the effort, it would pay off. I was honored to be considered a role model in academics, even though I had never had straight A's in my life, let alone straight 100% 's at the end of a semester.

It continued for the rest of my time at that school. I had found my rhythm. Over the last couple of years, I had watched my husband take classes and do homework as if it weren't a big deal. I hadn't ever experienced that type of anti-anxiety around school until now. Even in cosmetology, I didn't do this well on tests. I not only found something I was very interested in, but also learned how to study medical information thoroughly.

I crossed the stage on graduation day, among the few receiving the Director's Award. I was blown away by my own mental ability to call in a desire and place it in motion. I looked back on that first day at orientation and realized that a desire was planted in me to prove to myself, for the first time, that I was smart and driven, capable of doing big, scary things that I had been doubting because of my past and what people told me.

I had been asked to speak to that first class and inspire them with my experience. I was one of the few chosen to attend the 9 News Health Fair as a phlebotomy student and drew blood from hundreds of people. This would have never happened if I had fallen into the old story and put on the old cloak of "I am not smart enough." This would never have happened if I had listened to other people's opinions of me. This would never have happened if I hadn't followed through on the painful urge to better myself and shed the old identity I had adopted, thereby starting to break the seal on not caring as deeply about what others thought of me, knowing I was smart, talented, creative, and did well in school. My confidence expanded from a tiny balloon to a hot air balloon. I knew I was worth it, and I had something to offer!

The Lesson

As a people pleaser, you don't necessarily know how to stand firmly on your own inner knowings, so you easily fall victim to the ways of the "old you" or what people told you—you are not smart enough, pretty enough, or good enough. Instead of challenging that information, you wear it like an identity you have no control over, except that you CAN shed that piece of you and craft it into another story with a more beautiful design. That day, I learned I needed to shift my mentality and believe I could try, succeed, and that was all I needed to design the new me.

Reflection Questions

The identities we adopt often feel permanent, like the skin we were born with. But they're not. They're cloaks we can take off.

1. **What cloak of invisible identity are you wearing like it's your birthday suit?** One you have adopted: perhaps it's the "good girl," the "controller," or the "I'm not good enough."

2. **What can you start creating one craft at a time, changing your identity into something you never believed about yourself, yet really wanted to?**

3. So many people get stuck in the belief that they cannot change, and although change can be difficult and require taking different actions, it is possible and so worth removing the cloak. **What old story about yourself are you ready to shed?**

4. **What would it look/feel like to set your own standard—to show up for yourself in a way that proves the old story wrong?**

CHAPTER 22
IS IT TRENDY

Moving Closer to Work

Scott had found his first civilian aviation job and was driving an hour and fifteen minutes north every day. He continued doing this daily, sometimes spending two hours in the truck due to traffic. He had done this for the past three months while I was finishing my schooling. I was finally graduating, and our apartment lease was about to end for the year, which was good timing because we wanted to get closer to his work. We had a bit of savings and were feeling the itch to buy his second home and my first. We now knew we would need to move farther north, closer to his new job, outside the city, into a smaller town, and into a more country setting, which pleased both of us and was a Godsend.

We had been looking at a few houses, and neither of us minded buying a fixer-upper. I loved painting and decorating, and he was very handy, learning even more skills during our time together. We needed to find a short-term rental in this bustling college town. Well, we did. I found a sublease that would give us five more months to look for houses and for me to find a job in a medical clinic. We moved again. I had become an expert in packing by this time and left most of our stuff stacked in boxes blocking the sliding glass door in the tiny kitchen of a ground-level, disgusting, spider-infested apartment. I just kept reminding myself that this is temporary, and we took it day by day. Our house hunt was underway, and we were actively dreaming of the day we would get out of this nasty apartment.

The Job Search

Meanwhile, my job search was in motion, and I had an advantage in interview skills because I grew up in 4-H, where I learned sewing, cake decorating, woodworking, horse showing, pig showing, and rabbit showing. I was very familiar with the yearly project interviews on how to speak clearly and conduct myself well in anxiety-inducing settings. I actually had gotten every job I had interviewed for up until now, so I knew I just needed a shot.

It was now the days of submitting your resume to Never-Neverland in the computer abyss, not knowing if they actually reviewed it, and never getting to see who you were in person. I would send and send and not get a reply. Since I was a newbie in this industry, I knew I needed to take things into my own hands and think outside the box. We wanted to buy a house, and it would be better for our application if I had a job as well.

I printed a lot of resumes and cover letters, researched all the clinics around me that would need an MA, and showed up dressed professionally to hand my resume in person to the front desk. After a busy day doing that and wishing and hoping that it would be perfect timing for one of the companies, it was. A few days later, I got a call from a cosmetic dermatologist's office. The manager wanted to interview me and see if I was a good fit for one of his doctors. I was ecstatic—it was skin care!

I went to the interview, and while I was there, he scheduled a second interview, this time with the doctor I would be working with. It went well, and I was excited to work in a clinic that still made someone feel beautiful. I was offered a full-time position after the second interview.

Our First Home

I started working, and bippity boppity boo, we found a house. It was on a half-acre lot backing onto a quietish county road and was in foreclosure. It needed a lot of work, but the bank had already repainted the inside and replaced the carpet. The exterior needed a new paint job and lots of character and clean-up added, but the bones were there, and the rest could be changed. It was about 3,000 square feet and three stories. We were thrilled, and it felt huge.

I took a few days off a few months into my new job. We moved on a crisp fall day, and I will never forget the feeling in the air as we moved into a home we would get to settle into. The giant cottonwoods on the county road behind us were changing color. There was a brisk, cozy feeling as we packed the vehicles full at the dirty, infested college apartment and unloaded them into the beautiful house that was all ours. I couldn't wait to spend the winter getting to know it and making it our own.

The Botox Pressure

The following year, I fell in love with my job. I worked closely with the doctor and learned so much. I was her right-hand gal and helped intercept many of the questions she got most often, so she could focus on her genius. We became a good team with mutual respect. I worked at a clinic that offered Botox, skin care, lasers, bioidentical hormones, and more. Most of the women who worked there also used the service discount and often had Botox injected into their nearly non-existent wrinkled faces.

I was 27 at the time, with no wrinkles yet. They offered time and time again for me to start injecting, telling me that although I didn't have wrinkles, it would help prevent them. That made sense. When you freeze the muscle and tissue beneath, you prevent wrinkles because your skin cannot move normally. There was a 21-year-old who also worked at this clinic and took full advantage of the discount, getting Botox frequently. Still, my cowgirl hippie heart couldn't imagine doing that, not because I was afraid of needles—obviously not, I was a phlebotomist.

They didn't push, but they consistently recommended Botox. Every single employee from their 20s to their 60s was getting it done. I have nothing against Botox; someday, I might get it. I have wrinkles as I write this, but I am still inclined to follow my natural hippie heart into the abyss until I really need help. I am sure I'll wait so long the clinicians will tell me it's too late for my wrinkly Shar-Pei face, ha ha.

There I was, surrounded by this gorgeous group of women who worked out a ton, dressed well, had lasers and Botox done to stay looking sharp, and I was the only one not subscribing to that particular skin-care regimen. For the first time, I didn't care what they thought of me. I was here to do a job and to do it well. I was still young, and I had that going for my skin. I declined time after time, choosing myself for the first time in a group of powerful women who wanted to do the same thing to their faces.

This has nothing to do with Botox and everything to do with being in a group of women and choosing my own path, even if they don't understand or think it's the right move. It takes courage to say no to powerful women that you respect, especially if they have all jumped on the same path and are walking in the opposite direction from the path you are choosing. I didn't decide to follow. I knew the days of people-pleasing in a group of girls were coming to an end, and it felt SO liberating.

The Painting Party

It has now been solidified in my life at the time I write this book. I have had countless times in the past few years that I decided instead of going to the group get-together with friends, I would rather stay home, cuddle on the couch, or hang out with my family. Saying no to the girls' night out, even though I might "miss" something, doesn't even matter to me anymore.

Recently, I went to this sweet friend's birthday party, which was a painting class, and that is when I realized just how far I had come. She chose an adorable painting filled with girly colors—pinks, yellows, and purples. I was sitting next to her mom, and as the painting lady came along, we both quietly asked for just a drop of one or two more colors. We didn't want to dishonor the painting this friend and her daughter had chosen, but I personally wanted colors that would match my house. Just two drops of two different colors, and mine was completely different.

Part of me was thinking, "Oh crap, this is vastly different. I hope the birthday girl isn't angry," but I held the pose, knowing I felt so freaking good about the colors I'd chosen. It turns out she didn't care. A large photo was taken of all the gorgeous paintings that had been brought to life. She is a cherished girl, and it was extraordinary to be a part of her day and see the people who love her show up for her special celebration. When I look at that photo, my heart delights. I giggle because there I am, literally the black sheep in the crowd, going against the grain of a gorgeous, large, powerful group of women.

I didn't do anything wrong; I wasn't being disrespectful, but to me, it was a full-circle moment about who I was in my youth. It was a complete paradigm shift from the girl who followed her friends out into the hallway at high school, not knowing they had come up with an elaborate plan and had omitted me. I had a strong urge to be a follower back then, not in everything, but in enough things out of the fear of not being accepted. Now, sitting in this room with these incredible women, I felt the delight in my body ignite when I asked to go against the grain of what I was being served.

The Lesson

When you are part of a group doing the same thing, the people pleaser comes into play. The follower version raises her hand to participate so she doesn't have to feel FOMO (fear of missing out).

This doesn't happen to every people pleaser. There are different qualities of a people pleaser that I teach in my online courses, but this one can be sneaky and subtly intertwined. Many women find their voice around this issue in their early twenties, but our culture and public school upbringing are gasoline to this flame.

I want to ask these women, as their inflatable hand rises, "Do you really want that?" Could you close your eyes, tap into your own energy, and ask yourself whether this really excites you or if you're doing it because it's the latest trend and the environment around you?

I have learned that my spirit comes alive when I follow what lights me up versus "what I am supposed to do." It sparks an energy of aliveness that the people pleaser has no option but to leave.

This is incredibly important if you have a teenage girl you are raising: teach her how to tap into herself, keep pursuing the question, and remind her to come back to herself rather than what her peers are doing.

Reflection Questions

1. **Where would you rate yourself now?** Are you still going out at a time you don't want, hanging out in a group you don't really care about, to feel like you belong?

2. **Are you subscribing to something that everyone else is getting or doing because it is the trend?** What actually brings you joy in that thing?

3. **If you have a daughter, what are you showing and teaching her?** Are you modeling the courage to choose your own path?

4. **What, my love, are you saying to yourself when you go against the grain of what you desire?** What would you actually choose to do if you knew everything would be okay?

CHAPTER 23
JUDGMENT

Considering Parenthood

When I think back to our time in Vancouver, there was a moment when Scott and I first considered becoming parents. We were married and enjoying life, and I had to have an adjustment in birth control, or at least the realization that my body could no longer handle it. Naturally, it brought up the conversation of babies. I wasn't ready, but we were playing around with the "what ifs" and what it would be like. I had new friends who were moms and would speak to them about their experiences in child rearing.

I had one friend who had been my boss at the bank when I was a teller right out of high school. She was ten years older than me, had three boys, and was at home taking care of them rather than working. I remember calling her one day to talk about what it was like to have children. Of course, I also spoke to my own mother about this, but I needed to calibrate to someone who was raising the current generation. Her conversation with me left me standing where I had started. She was candid, and I have always loved that about this friend; she walks to the beat of her own drum and lets whatever she's thinking out of her mouth. It is delightful.

We had a long conversation, and it was basically summed up as "Being a mom is the best and hardest job you will ever do." It left me confused, with the pros and cons balancing each other out. I was dipping my toe into the possibility of becoming a mom. It wasn't something that beckoned at my heart like a loud siren alerting me that it was time. I had never been the girl who wanted ten kids, yet I had never thought that I wouldn't have children. Either way, when the subject came up, I felt frozen and unqualified in my body. Deep thoughts ran wild through my head, asking, "Can I do that? Am I qualified?"

It is a ton of responsibility bringing a human into this world, even if my name Rachel literally means "motherly," so I put it on the back burner. I carried an enormous respect for motherhood, and I wasn't sure I was capable of the job.

The Decision to Try

Flash forward. We both had good jobs, and our hearts were delighted to settle into a new home that was all ours. On the weekends, we spent our time fixing it up and strengthening our "elbow grease with some sweat equity." The last year with school, moving, job hunts, and home buying was sprinkled with "what if" thoughts again—thoughts about what it would look like to add a baby to our family. It was slightly different this time, and I knew I was ready, though I still felt overwhelmed by the responsibility of caring for another human being. This time, I felt deep knowing that I wanted to try.

Let me be clear: "Hi, I'm Rachel, a responsible, people-pleasing extrovert." There was no reason I shouldn't have a baby; I did all the "right" things and sacrificed like it was my job. It was my own doubt and voices telling me, "I don't know if I would be a good mother," that held me back. Stronger, however, there was a deep knowing that felt supported, as if divine energy were radiating and drawing me into the adventure of motherhood. So, we went down the rabbit hole, trying to get pregnant.

I thought it would be easy. My body didn't have to adjust to shifting hormones, as I have been off birth control and using natural timing to prevent pregnancy for a couple of years now. My mother often says, "Your father looked at me, and I was pregnant." Yeah, she is one of those "fertile myrtles" out there who got pregnant easily. She had a couple of things that were hard during her pregnancies, but, relatively speaking, she had good pregnancies. So, I expected mine to be that easy.

We hadn't been "trying," but we hadn't been protecting. It had been a few months, and nothing had happened, so we started getting more serious. If you have ever "tried" to get pregnant, you know what I am talking about. It goes from skipping around and lightly thinking "I'm trying to get pregnant" to full force "I need to get pregnant." At least for me, it did. There was an encroaching panic as I realized that eight months of trying had shown it might be more complicated than I thought, and now I couldn't get the baby off my mind.

The Miscarriage

We were scheduled to drive home to our family's house for Christmas in a month. It was just before Thanksgiving, my period hadn't shown up, so I took a test, and it was positive. I couldn't believe it. Perhaps we would tell them that at Christmas, it would be the perfect Christmas gift. In the middle of the night, eight weeks from my last period, I started bleeding. There was no pain, no warning, just blood. I was met with a tender embrace from my husband as I slipped into my clothes to go to work.

It was a quiet car ride as we sat in sadness, knowing this wasn't the one. A deep grief came over me and made me wonder if I was even going to get the chance to create a life in my body. I was a healthy person, someone who took care of herself. I didn't drink alcohol, only twice a year at the most, and I had never smoked anything. I worked out somewhat consistently and ate mainly whole foods. I was confused and so unbelievably disappointed. A cloud of shame hung over me as I had thoughts of what was wrong with my body.

The Doctor's Kindness

I arrived at work that day, buttoned up my emotions, and dove into my job. I could feel the doctor I worked directly with watching me out of the corner of her eye. She had three children and came from a large family with kids all around her. I wasn't crying; I hadn't thought I was acting differently, but she gently walked over to me and stood. Her presence and warmth were enough to make my nostrils flare, and my lips tremble. She looked at me with her large, deep brown eyes and said softly, "Are you ok?"

That was all it took. I was being held and seen for something I thought was so hidden. I hadn't told a soul we were trying to have a baby—no one, none of our families, friends, or coworkers. She was a mom, aunt, sister, daughter, and doctor; she had Jedi Knight baby skills, and I burst into tears. She immediately pulled me into her arms like a mother with a child and held me. I was finally able to speak through the blubbering that was pouring out of me, that I had just had a miscarriage and was actively bleeding. She cried with me. She gave me such comfort that day and sent me home to process in whatever way I needed. I will never forget her kindness during this tough time in my life; she was an angel in disguise that day.

Christmas and the Secret

We went home that Christmas, joyful to see my family, but not ready to share and process with them. Not because they wouldn't hold a deep care, love, and compassion, but because it had been nearly five years since Scott and I had married, and although they didn't pressure us at all, I knew they were dying inside waiting for the day we said we were pregnant. I wanted so much more to surprise them than to be held in this moment of grief. Scott held me, we held each other, and we honored the little life that tried to come but couldn't.

Trying Again

Now the desire to have a baby was pulsing through my veins; it's all I wanted. After Christmas, I ripped off the band-aid of my gut issues. I went entirely gluten-free, and we started trying again. After a week or so of everything feeling normal in my body, I couldn't resist my handsome hubby anymore, and off we went, with hope still in my heart and a busy work schedule ahead of me after the holidays.

January slipped away quickly, and February was upon us. It was the week of Valentine's Day, and I was contemplating how we would celebrate. As I looked at the calendar, I had been so busy I hadn't noticed that I was late, really late, days late. I am a very consistent person when it comes to my cycle, and it was off. I grabbed a handy-dandy preggo-my-eggo test and used it. I didn't want to get my hopes up. I didn't want to worry about this one going wrong. Would it take? Would it last? Would my body support it? Would it even be positive? It had been a solid year since we had started trying, and I was a snail in this baby-making business.

My heart dropped. I felt a bulge in my throat. The tears welled up, and I started to bawl, hitting my knees on the ground, thanking God for another chance with a positive pregnancy stick.

The Valentine's Day Surprise

I wanted to burst into the other room and run screaming through the house that it was positive, but then a thought arose: Valentine's Day was two days away. Oh, the agony wailed through my body. Could I wait two days to tell the father of my child? Yes, come to find out, I love to surprise people more than blurt things out. Most of my creations have been done in private. A well of energy builds in my body, bouncing around, propelling something into creation. I couldn't wait to surprise him with the most magnificent Valentine's gift.

Valentine's Day morning finally arrived, and we were getting ready for work. I was in the bathroom and asked him to come to me. I reached my hand out, holding a gift bag. He looked at me, smiled, and said "thanks" as he leaned over to kiss me. He said, "Happy Valentine's Day." He pulled out a cute white ruffled onesie with the word "Daddy" on it. His eyes flew open. "REALLY," he said in surprised delight, and tears leaked down my cheeks as I nodded my head. We embraced, not wanting to let go of each other or the moment.

The Lesson

This was my journey into becoming a mother. My mother and I are incredibly close, but it was my body, my heart, my womb. I wasn't ready to share. There were days of doubt, days of wanting to dial her number, hear her voice, and cry on the phone. Days I felt so much guilt as a people pleaser, worried about her judgment of my decision to keep the miscarriage to myself. I fought the urge to tell her because I knew it wasn't for the right reason; it was to please her, out of concern she'd be upset that I wasn't sharing a tough time. I didn't tell her when I knew we were so close to surprising them with the best gift of life. I chose to fight against what was right for someone else and instead stay steady on the path of what was right for me, my husband, and our journey. It was hard, but I held steady, not wanting to give it to others for judgment or understanding just yet.

Reflection Questions

Sometimes the most loving thing you can do is keep something sacred until you're ready to share it.

1. **Are you revealing things about yourself that you aren't ready to share in fear that it might hurt the other person's feelings by not divulging?** Do you feel pressure to share because they would not want you to walk alone?

2. **Or the opposite: Do you not share your inner hurt and really need to voice it to heal?** Do you need to speak with someone about something you have been going through, and you are worried about their judgment?

3. **Do you need them to listen, without forming an opinion?** Are you afraid they will judge you if you let them in? Could you preface this talk with "I don't need advice, I just need someone to listen?"

4. **What are you holding close to your heart right now that you're not ready to share?** Can you permit yourself to keep it sacred for as long as you need?

Section
THREE

—·—

UNTAMED

CHAPTER 24
CHOOSING ME

_T_his was the moment I learned that choosing yourself isn't selfish—it's survival. And sometimes the universe has to force your hand to show you what you've been too afraid to claim on your own. For me, that force came in the form of a baby who made me unemployable to everyone but her. And thank God for it.

Morning Sickness Arrives

I had an upcoming adventure: traveling with my husband on his work trip and taking the week off to explore Vancouver, BC. He had a lot of meetings to be in at a significant event his company holds each year, and it was an excellent opportunity for me to hang out in a lavish hotel room, rest, and explore Canada, a country I hadn't been to.

Upon week seven, the pregnancy let me know it was on board. I was in the middle of a laser treatment, assisting the doctor I worked under. I looked at her intensely and said, "Excuse me," as I ran out of the room and down the hall to the bathroom. I slammed the door behind me, and lunch left my body. Morning sickness had arrived, except it wasn't "morning" sickness; it was all-day, all-night, no matter what I ate or did, sickness. I learned really quickly which foods taste the same when they come back up. Bananas and orange juice were the best.

It kept getting worse. I was weak and couldn't keep anything down. I tried to work for days, but I felt terrible. I didn't mind the throwing up; what I did mind was the non-stop nausea. It never ceased. It was so hard. The doctor I worked for reassured me that this baby would stick, that it most likely wouldn't miscarry due to its undertaking on my body—not that that's true in every case—but it really helped me to rest assured that I had a little miracle on the way. Well, that little miracle was definitely committed and was taking my lunch money daily.

I ended up having to call in on pregnancy week eight because I couldn't stop throwing up and was so weak. I tried keeping myself hydrated, but it didn't work well, and I ended up in the hospital with an IV. It helped me rehydrate, and they gave me medication to help with the constant nausea, which kept it at bay and slowed the vomiting. For the entire pregnancy, I never stopped throwing up multiple times a day and lived with a nausea that wouldn't leave. I tried every natural substance I could that might help; sometimes it relieved it for a while, but not long. I continued working full-time, going from sitting and entering information for the doctor to standing and assisting her with procedures. I had gotten used to this new way of feeling, and there wasn't a glow for me; it was pregnancy survival, but I was up for the challenge. On the weekends and evenings, I crashed. I was so tired; getting laundry done was my only goal.

The Easter Surprise

We told our families at the three-month mark, which made us feel better about the survival rate. Scott's parents and family were notified over the phone since they lived states away, and we were able to surprise my parents in person on Easter when they came to visit. I knew I didn't have it in me to host Easter, but I knew it would be hell for me to get in a car already nauseous to drive and see them. So we invited them to share a meal and celebrate together. Of course, they were delighted. They arrived on a Friday after we had worked all week, cleaned house, and bought food they might want for Easter dinner. I knew my mom would gladly help me prepare the meal. I hadn't started showing yet, except maybe a tiny bump that I already had on my tummy.

We welcomed them into our home. Petrie needed her full five minutes of first-child greetings, then we sat them down to give them a gift bag for Easter. They opened it and pulled out one large, tall male bunny, a tall female bunny, and then a little tiny baby bunny. That was it; it took them no time, and they began questioning, with tears in their eyes. We confirmed their thoughts, and the tears started to pour. I'll never forget what they said next, joking, "We thought you guys didn't know how to make a baby. We've waited for so long." Laughter and embarrassment radiated through the house.

Thank goodness, as I predicted, my mom took over and cooked the Easter meal, while I tried to help where I could and spent a lot of that time in the restroom trying to hold it all in. We got the opportunity to share the whole story with them, and their hearts were forever changed.

My mother finally understood why I hadn't called much or been available to talk a lot the past few months. I chose myself. I chose to put myself first for the first time because even speaking was hard to do with that amount of nausea trying to erupt out of my throat. They were understanding and couldn't believe all that had happened. I do empathize with my mom and her not knowing what I was going through; that would be really tough as a mom, but I had my eye on the goal of their surprise, and it was so worth it!

The Blood Clot

The pregnancy continued throughout the summer, and my husband and I took small breaks from yard work on weekends to prepare the nursery. The due date was getting closer. I wasn't feeling too nervous—just very anxious to get this precious baby here—and had even forgotten what it felt like not to be nauseous. We found out it was a girl—surprisingly—and she was due in October. Fall is an excellent time for me; it's my birthday, when we bought our home, and now, when I would welcome a new soul into this world.

I was five weeks from my delivery, and work was trucking along. One night after work, I went home, and my left leg felt uncomfortable and more noticeable than usual. It seemed tighter than the right one. I decided to lie down and elevate it. As the night went on, the pain started to set in, and it was beyond uncomfortable, so I called into the nurses' hotline. She advised me to continue doing what I was doing and, if it got worse, to go in—perhaps I had just tweaked something.

The next day, my husband and I carpooled to work. He dropped me off, and by lunch, he was picking me up to drive five minutes across the freeway. My leg was swelling. It was in pain and slightly turning a purple-blue color. Something was definitely wrong. We went into the ER, and they triaged me immediately. An ultrasound was performed to look for a blood clot. The technician went all the way up my leg into the crease of my groin. She found nothing. They dismissed me from the hospital that evening and sent us home with similar instructions.

Except overnight, it got worse, and the pain was unbearable. I couldn't put much weight on it. I went back to the ER, and this time they followed the vein up above my hips. Bingo. They found not one but two blood clots. They immediately admitted me and started giving me heparin and putting circulation massagers on my legs, among other things.

I was scared. What the heck, first off, it was apparent that something was wrong with my leg for anyone with two eyes to see the swelling and discoloration, so I knew it wasn't good. Secondly, I was afraid of what would happen. Would the baby be ok, especially with all this medication coursing through my blood, and would I survive?

Scott called my parents and told them the news once all was figured out, and I was admitted. It was later in the afternoon, and little did we know they had rushed home from their jobs, thrown stuff in their truck, and drove all night to get to us. It was early the next morning. I was waking up in the hospital, and they came walking into my room. Again, the tears came seeping out, in complete comfort to have more people I deeply loved there to support this scary moment in my life.

Managing the Crisis

The doctor got the clot stabilized after two nights and sent me home. The pain was better, yet not gone, and my leg had started to look more normal. The ick part was that I now had to inject my stomach with a dose of heparin daily to ensure we kept the clot stabilized and not traveling. It was a lot to get my brain wrapped around. I would inject in the morning when my husband was gone for work, and he would inject in my back in the evenings. It was brutal, not because of the needle but the thought of the medication and putting a needle in my belly, close to a baby that was almost ready to hatch. It seemed counterintuitive for a mother desiring a healthy baby. Still, there was no way around it; I wanted to survive. I remember thinking how I knew blood clots were scary, but no one ever talked about how painful they could be.

The Decision to Stay Home

I tried to work the next week, but my new hematologist and high-risk OB advised otherwise. They knew I had been hard at it, not wanting to ask for a bit of rest and time off, and met my resistance with stern words about the baby's and my well-being for the next five weeks. It was time to fight something that was raging a war in my body, time to tell my doctor, who I had loved working with, and the manager, who was a workaholic, that I wouldn't be returning, and the date I thought I would end work was now moved up five weeks sooner.

Luckily, we had been training another MA to take my spot temporarily while I was on maternity leave, but really, Scott and I had decided to keep me home as a stay-at-home mom. The doctor I worked for, of course, asked me about my plan, but I couldn't tell her. There was a sense of obligation to return, especially since we had become a well-oiled machine in how we worked together; it was a seamless flow of understanding each other's needs.

For months, I tortured myself with impossible questions: Could I work from home? Could I still serve her somehow? Could I be the employee she needed AND the mother I wanted to be? Listen to that. Listen to how the people pleaser in me was STILL trying to serve everyone else first, even with a baby growing inside me. My heart knew the answer. I wanted to be home. I wanted to be the mom who got to stay home and attend mommy-and-me classes, like I had seen my aunt do. I wanted to witness every moment, every milestone, every first. I didn't want to split myself in two—half at work, half at home, never fully present anywhere.

But the people pleaser? She was having her death throes. She was screaming, "You can't disappoint her! She relies on you! What will she think? The collective says moms work. You need to help pay bills. Staying home is unacceptable!" The woman I was becoming had a different answer: "My baby relies on me more.

The blood clot forced my hand—but it also forced my freedom.

I had to tell her. And as I walked toward that conversation, I felt the old me reaching for apologies, scrambling for ways to soften the blow, to make it easier for HER. The people-pleaser was gasping, trying to find the right words to minimize my own needs.

But something was different this time. Even as I approached her with that familiar mousy, meek demeanor—even as the apologies started spilling out—I knew: I was done negotiating my own life.

She looked at me strangely. And then she congratulated me.

The monster I had built in my imagination—the disappointment, the anger, the destroyed relationship—it never existed. The people-pleaser had lied to me. Again. But this time, I saw the lie for what it was.

She would miss me, but of course, was so happy I would be there for my daughter and have this special time she also took when she had young children.

I was surprised. Something I had fought against, out of fear of not pleasing someone else, for months, was met with a pleasant surprise of gratitude and celebration. She adored babies and asked several times to watch my little one for a few hours while Scott and I went on a date. That didn't happen for many months, but we continued a sweet friendship after I left the clinic.

Gracie's Arrival

I was induced due to the blood clot one week earlier than her due date. It was, as any birth is, intense and magical. We welcomed our baby girl, Gracie, into this world, and as I held her in my arms, I felt an overwhelming sense of immense protection and responsibility that frightened and enlightened me at the same time. She was here; her little soul made it into my arms, and I would never be the same.

The Lesson

I was standing at a crossroads, and I could see both paths clearly.

One led to my mother's story: the woman who returned to work because she thought she had to, who loved her children fiercely but couldn't say no to the grind. I wasn't judging her—I was learning from her.

The other path was unknown. Terrifying. But mine.

I chose the unknown. I chose myself. And in doing so, I cracked a generational pattern wide open.

I wanted to go to mommy-and-me classes, change all her diapers, be submerged in all her expressions, stay home, and bake. It was fall after all, and that is when baking gets ramped up in my heart. Thank heavens, the moment I had her, the nausea dissipated just like that. It was shocking, and now, I had all the cravings and desires to make delicious food.

I wanted to experience this tiny human, and I couldn't imagine being one of the moms who had to drop her off at a daycare at 3 months old. I feel so deeply for those mothers and what they must go through; it must be like having your heart ripped out of your chest and beaten. I say that from my perspective. I realize a lot of moms want to go back to work; they have worked really hard to get to where they are in their companies, and they love their jobs—it is a part of them. I respect whatever your decision is; either way has its perks and costs.

The people-pleaser screamed that I would disappoint someone who relied on me. But here's what I finally understood:

Your employer can replace you in two weeks. Your baby cannot. Your family cannot. You are irreplaceable to the people who matter most—but only if you show up for them. And showing up for them means choosing YOU first. Not selfishly. Strategically. Powerfully.

A depleted, people-pleasing mother serves no one—least of all herself.

Reflection Questions

The fear of disappointing others can lead us to make decisions that run counter to what our hearts truly want.

1. **Where or when, my dear, have you made a huge life decision that wasn't what you wanted because you felt the pressure of displeasing the other person?** How did that decision work out?

2. **What did you learn from that experience?** Did that person actually react the way you had built it up in your head, or did they take it like it was a given?

3. **Are you currently facing a decision where you're prioritizing someone else's needs or expectations over what you deeply desire?** What would it look like to choose yourself?

4. An employer can replace you, but a baby and family cannot. **Where else in your life does this principle apply?**

CHAPTER 25
DON'T RUN

This chapter is about the moment I learned to hold the pose.

The people-pleaser wanted me to run—back to work, back to earning my worth, back to proving I was enough through a paycheck. The unworthiness was deafening. But I didn't run. I planted my feet and let it crash against me until it broke.

Here's what that looked like.

Alone with Gracie

A few days later, Gracie and I were at home, trying to get into a sleep schedule. My hormones were now crashing since they had no baby to build any longer. She was only four days old, and my parents had to return home to their jobs. Scott also had to return to work on Monday. I was facing the reality of being alone with this tiny, itty-bitty human all by myself while also still managing a blood clot. I was terrified.

I wanted more than anything in the world to keep Gracie safe, and I was also so worried about doing everything right with the blood clot instructions. I was now on Lovenox, another blood thinner that also had me injecting in my belly or side for the next six weeks. I was bruised everywhere and felt and looked like a pincushion. It didn't matter. Although I was nervous that the blood clot might break free and travel, I wouldn't let my brain meander to those thoughts for very long. I spent what felt like hours a day gazing at Gracie, thinking, Wow, we did it—we got her here safely. She was a perfect dark-haired, blue-eyed, red-lipped beauty. She was magnificent. I couldn't believe we had created life—a being with a soul, a beating heart, and eyes that magnetized me. She was so feminine that the nurses kept saying how beautiful and girly her little face was. She was perfect.

The Letdown

Monday morning came, and I was left alone. I was so let down that my mom wouldn't and couldn't stay longer. She would've stayed longer, but she and her brothers were in the midst of selling one of their main businesses, and again, she was the only one in the accounting department. She did things the old-school way and didn't bring a laptop. I was weepy, my hormones crashed, and I was so disappointed that she wasn't here to teach me what the heck to do with this tiny, fragile, now earthly being. I was genuinely scared.

I had light postpartum sadness that ran its course for a few weeks. Thank goodness it was short, because that is some serious doom and gloom. My heart goes out to the mothers whose postpartum depression lasts for months and beyond. Pregnancy is truly one of the biggest miracles of our time. I believe that our modern society makes it easy to fall into the belief that pregnancy and birth are "so easy." For some moms, it is; for others, it is one of their life's most significant conquests.

Nowadays, there are so many ways to get pregnant and have a baby, and it seems like everyone around pops out kids like bread popping up from a toaster. I want to acknowledge that pregnancy is a true marvel. Your womb creates life, and even if you had to go another route to get your baby, your womb is still full of magical life-producing energy, even if your journey looked different. Pregnancy is tough on your body, yet God's energy within you knows how to grow this tiny human from the cells and DNA you and your partner share. It is truly a modern-day phenomenon that sometimes gets overlooked. Due to the remarkable advances in modern technology and medicine, we have seen so many developments that we can easily forget how mysterious our spiritual body technology remains.

There was a moment during my pregnancy—again, maybe from the hormones—I imagined her coming out covered in hair, but she wasn't; she was perfect. My womb knew what to do, how to create tiny arms, legs, fingers, and toes. It will always be a magical, divine mystery to me.

Finding My Way

Looking back now, I understand my mom's position, but in the moment, she did what she knew best—and, although she was in love with this new tiny human, work was bigger than her "no." It hurts to think of how desperately I needed her at that time. I do believe God had other plans for me, plans that he wanted me to rely on my own motherly skills and let those kick in. I do believe it was the right call for my mom to return to work. Gracie and I took tiny baby steps together in this new world, alone at home. I could've used more support from someone going through the exact moment of the newborn phase. I had joined a MOPS group while I was at home those last few weeks before Gracie was born, and had made some sweet friends with children. A few stopped by and brought a life-giving meal. It was incredibly kind, but the only one I could really relate to had children who were six months old and one who was about three. She was seasoned. She was confident. She just laughed and giggled when I wanted to cry and ask if she was feeling the same. She was not. We were having an entirely different experience at this moment.

I felt so alone, even though I was a phone call away from getting support from my family. I called my mom or googled anything weird I experienced, which was a lot, because this was all brand new to me, and that can be really scary for the brain. I wanted someone who was walking a relatable path while caring for a young newborn. As I write this, my OG bestie has started this movement. She had her second child eight years ago and had a really hard postpartum after a terrifying birth. She has started an organization in her local town that brings mothers together to share their sacred experience of giving birth and walking those first few months together. It's brilliant. It bonds these women and makes them feel deeply heard, seen, and relatable when they need it most. She is doing her heart's work, and I couldn't be more proud of her cause.

Settling In

My mom was crushed; she couldn't stand the fact that she couldn't be there for me and to hold this baby she wanted to claim as her own. However, there was too much work, so she and my dad made a point of coming up every two months for the entire time we lived in that area. It was special, and we really enjoyed having them around.

It was winter now, and Gracie was a couple of months old. I was going to MOPS meetings and my twice-a-week check-in, as I was now on Coumadin and had to go into a clinic for them to prick me and evaluate my blood. Gracie and I would go on short walks in the afternoon if it were decently warm on a wintery day. Scott's mom came out to meet Gracie five weeks after she was born and celebrate Thanksgiving with us. I was settling into this new routine, and it felt good.

The "Not Enough" Plague

I felt so unbelievably blessed and spoiled. I was driving a car I had coveted for a few years prior, and we had bought it used when I was about 6 months pregnant. I had a beautiful, safe, comfortable home, a husband who supported us—I was living out the fantasy of being a stay-at-home mom. This should be a time of pure joy, no worries. Why did this feeling keep popping up? This feeling of not being enough—of not doing enough, of not contributing enough. Enough kept coming to mind in every possible way.

Scott made plenty of money at his job. We had enough to cover bills and save a bit. We weren't strapped so tightly that it was hard or stressful, yet "I wasn't doing enough" kept repeating in my head, plaguing me with the idea that I wasn't contributing financially. Oh, this was hard. I would be doing fine for a while, and then a random squirrel would run through my head, terrorizing all the peaceful birds enjoying their day. Of course, I would follow that squirrel down the path, down the path of "you are not making money, therefore you are not worthy."

I gag writing that sentence now. But back then? It was my daily torture.

I was doing the most important and hardest job in the world—and the people-pleaser told me it didn't count. No paycheck, no worth. That was the lie I had been taught my whole life.

The shame clawed at me. I wasn't earning. I wasn't contributing. The old programming ran on repeat, trying to drag me back to the familiar prison.

But I didn't run. I held the damn pose. And slowly, painfully, I began to rewrite the lie.

Trauma from my previous relationship came barreling in, reminding me of a time when I believed that my worth as a woman was because I paid for things. Thank God I found balance in this new relationship with my husband. But there was still a deep remnant in my soul from that relationship and from watching my mom, subconsciously, show me what a woman should do: work. Work even if it tears you up because you miss your child's activities, work even when your children need more of you, and work even when you have a new grandbaby in the world.

Let me be clear, this is a selfish first-world desire, or at least a long-forgotten memory of what I knew should've been. A lot of women don't have their moms, or aren't in a relationship with her any longer, and would be unbelievably ecstatic if their moms could spend those first few days with them and the newborn. At that time, I wanted more. It was a recurring theme that weaved through our loving, marvelous, humorous, and caring best-friend, mother-daughter relationship. Her theme was: "I love my children so much I could eat them, yet I deeply cannot unsee the work that I need to accomplish." This was the battle that ran the show.

I was shown that your worth as a woman is measured by how hard you can work—not because anyone said so, but because that was the behavior I was repeatedly shown.

Choosing to Stay

I had multiple conversations with my husband about financial contributions over a couple of years as we raised Gracie. Yes, of course, two incomes are better than one. Still, I married a man whose providership coursed through his veins. This man knew the importance of keeping me with our child and that it would be better at the time than a larger savings. He was growing prouder every year, saying he had the honor of providing for a stay-at-home wife.

As most stay-at-home moms know, there is the financial piece, and then there is the brain piece—the mental piece, when you are so delighted to talk about something other than just baby talk, the part of you that realizes that at one time you were a woman with a full-fledged life. I have watched many mothers come and go at this "stay at home" reality, most of them disappearing into the abyss of work again, afraid they would lose themselves, and thought they were going batshit crazy, having to cater to a tiny little human and forgoing the life they had before. It's not easy on either side of the coin. My advice has always been to choose the lesser evil for yourself and your family.

As I write this, Gracie will be 13 next month. I have stuck to the path I have fully committed to: being a stay-at-home mom. For a year and a half, I worked part-time only while she was in preschool; on the days she was home, I was home. It has been a journey of creation and healing within myself as I have raised her. I didn't just sit at home, focusing entirely on her—I mean, I did, but the other 10% of my time, we flipped two houses, I decorated and planted up a storm, and I got to introduce her to so many animals and crafts and play with her over and over and over. Then, if my mind wasn't satisfied, instead of submitting to the thought of going back to work, I started healing. I started pouring into books and topics, and self-help power-up avenues. I say "pour"; however, it was only for a few minutes a day because this little human was a spitfire of busyness and delight.

We have had music classes together since she was three, have dressed up and danced in the living room three hundred times, and have sung along to Frozen, who knows how many times. I created a comforting homecoming for my husband with a meal ready on the table, a clean house, and a toddler bathed and prepared for daddy time. It was magical. I still fought the worthiness thoughts from time to time, but I kept choosing Gracie—and, in turn, choosing myself. I allowed the space to dive into new concepts and heal so many scars from the past, changing how I thought about and saw the world. Little did I know it was God setting the stage, helping me put one foot in front of the other, and continuing to teach me the lessons I had to learn, powering me up for the reason my soul landed here.

The Lesson

Don't run.

The people-pleaser wants you to flee back to safety—back to the desk, the paycheck, the external proof of your worth. She will whisper that you're not contributing, not earning, not enough.

Don't listen to her. She's dying, and she's desperate.

Hold the pose. Let the unworthiness crash against you like waves against a cliff. You are not running anymore. You are standing. And every moment you stand is another crack in her grip on you.

If I had listened to my doubt—if I had run—I wouldn't have what I have today. A daughter I laugh with every single day. Conversations that go deep, that matter, that heal us both.

The people-pleaser didn't want me to have this. She wanted me back at a desk, proving my worth to strangers.

I'm so glad I let her die.

Reflection Questions

Whether you are a mother or not, you can still apply this.

1. **Have you been feeling like you are not enough, you are not contributing enough?** Yet deep in your soul, you know you are doing the right thing, withstanding the resistance? If so, where is that happening in your life, and how do you want to move forward with the larger picture in mind?

2. If you are a stay-at-home mom who is contemplating going back to work, I ask you one question: **What would you create at home with your children that would satisfy your intellect, possibly your pocketbook, and your soul as you raise your kids?**

3. **Where are you running from an uncomfortable feeling instead of holding the pose?** What would happen if you stayed? What would be the worst-case scenario—and is it really as big as you think?

CHAPTER 26
THE WORLD IS LOUD

This is where I learned the difference between pushing my way through life and flowing through it.

For years, I had been running on wounded masculine energy—white-knuckling, proving, performing. I thought that was strength. It wasn't. It was exhaustion dressed up as productivity.

The real power? It came when I learned to stop pushing and start receiving.

Gracie was now about 14 months old, and I had started to accept that I was worthy despite not having a paying "job." The feeling still plagued me here and there, and the collective belief that women were supposed to do it all was strong. My husband and I sometimes joke that I run circles around him. We are both incredibly forward-moving, productive human beings, but moms are a whole other beast. Women are fierce, badass caregivers, kind, soft, seductive, part feminine, part masculine, embodied leaders, get-it-done'rs, up all night with kids, nurturers, and we carry the magic of creation itself within our bodies. We are multi-dimensional creatures, ever-changing and in motion.

I was speaking with Scott recently, and we had a long laugh about a funny comment he made. He said, "he literally just figured me out and was creating the manual," and then I went and blew the manual out of the water and changed. It had us laughing for a while.

Understanding Masculine and Feminine Energy

Masculine energy and men desperately want a manual on women; we are complex. The feminine changes her mind often—not in a flighty way—but the true embodied feminine drips with pleasure and shifts toward her desires. She embodies new skills and awakens old memories, becoming who she is meant to be. She is like a river flowing down the mountain, ever changing. When truly embodied, she is one of the most steady and potent energies out there. She can command what she desires while holding pure love, softness, and warmth for those around her.

The masculine is the bank of the river, the strong, steady, ever-consistent boundary that holds and contains the water of the feminine. It isn't meant to quiet her; it is intended to support her, carry her, and allow her to ebb and flow the way she sees fit. Men mainly carry masculine energy with a touch of feminine, and women mainly carry feminine energy with a touch of masculine. This isn't how you dress; it's the energy that emanates from you, and how you give and receive from life.

This is completely and dramatically changed or shifted as you learn lessons and are taught things as you grow up. It is very natural to now see men in their feminine with a very masculine wife. Childhood conditioning created those shifts. Those two people married because polarity was necessary for attraction. If it works for you and you don't mind playing the energetic switch, then great. If you are miserable in your relationship, I would start by looking at the types of energy you both have running and learn how to get back into your energetic match. One of you will have to be feminine and the other masculine to create polarity, attraction, and sexual energy within your relationship. If you don't have that polarity, you will end up in a roommate situation or find yourself butting heads often. This will take time and require guidance and understanding of what those roles carry.

The Wounded Masculine Woman

I know this woman. I WAS this woman.

When a woman is in her wounded masculine, trying to please everyone and do everything she possibly can, she becomes a bull in a china shop. She can't slow down. She can't receive. She proves her worth through exhaustion and calls it strength.

But it's not strength. It's a cage she built herself.

She has to work, she loves to-do lists and really tight schedules, and she commands everyone in sight about what they will do. She has an intense moving-forward energy and is on the verge of a burnout because she is burning through more testosterone than her actual body produces; therefore, she is about to or already has created an autoimmune disease. I have an entire course for her to help her get back into her body and use her femininity as a strength. It is called Vibrational Bliss on my website.

I don't blame women for getting into this mode; I completely understand it, because I went through it during the beginning of motherhood. To clarify for those badass women who are running mainly in the masculine reading this, telling me to eff off if I try to slow them down, it's not about slowing down all the time. There is a flow state where you get as much done, if not more, and you do it in pleasure, not out of push. I will not slow down. I have always been a fast mover, but you have to ask yourself, "Who are you being in that fast-moving action?"

Are you in your feminine flow state—buzzing, connected to source and creation, and it's pouring out of you as you light up people around you? Or are you yelling, pushing, shoving, and verbally commanding people to do the things you want, white-knuckling your way there, proving your worth? I had to unlearn decades of conditioning to get here. The people-pleaser thrived in that wounded masculine—always doing, never receiving, earning worth through work.

Breaking free meant learning a new way to move through the world.

When you are in the feminine flow state and are connected to Source energy, everything around you moves with ease. It doesn't mean everything always goes perfectly, yet you learn to dance, nurture not only yourself but also the people around you, and move through the next obstacle easily. When I focus on getting more in touch with the divine, my body, and listening to the subtle cues of my intuition, I am not burnt out. I am actually waking up earlier, thinking of all the pleasures in my day—pleasures that might be me working, running my daughter around, helping her with schoolwork, or conjuring up a new way to seduce my husband. When you take care of your feminine needs, you can make anything pleasurable. At the same time, the overflow from your radiant energy pours out naturally to other people with no effort.

This doesn't just happen overnight, but if you find yourself attracting more feminine energy from men, men you work harder than, and you are consistently barking at them to "do" things, my love, you are in the masculine. He has stepped into the feminine, not realizing it. If you are both running strong on your masculinity, there will typically be a lot of tug-of-war and fighting at home, both of you trying to prove that you are more worthy or that you have it harder in some way. If you have both stepped into your feminine, then nothing really gets done—R and R is all you both want. In both of these cases, the sexual tension will be removed, and the polarity no longer exists.

Women were never meant to be focused like the masculine all the time; we get to do the thing and make it look and feel like it is dripping with ease and pleasure. This takes time to course-correct, and by no means am I stating that the masculine gets to have power over the feminine. The masculine instead gets to hold the feminine in her badass mission.

The Balance We Need

I know there are a lot of women who hate men. I agree that when women had no rights, we needed a movement, a voice, and equal rights. I am so unbelievably grateful to the women who paved the way in the feminist era. However, the pendulum has swung to the opposite side, and we need it to balance out. As times change, we need to re-evaluate how far it needs to go and what still serves or needs to change.

There are many women out there who are man-haters. As much as I see that they have fear running the show for what a man can and cannot do in their lives, I also understand that, unfortunately, these women have been taught or shown most of the traits of a wounded masculine man or a predator. They have forgotten or never seen how the true masculine can help them.

Proper, healthy masculine men will support you while you heal and not be intimidated when you have large dreams. They don't keep you down and tell you your place in the home is to cook and clean, unless that is what you want. They support your dreams, provide for you even if you make more than them—it's an energy—and have your back, making you feel protected as fuck. They don't trash-talk you to their friends, and they know that your success also has to do with how they lead in their masculine. It is a divine interwoven balance. They will still misstep sometimes, just as you will, especially if you are both learning.

When you marry the right person, you will trigger the crap out of each other at first, as they are meant to heal some of the wounds within you. If you need counseling or mentorship while you work through these, then get it. Do not sit there and trash-talk the other person. When you feel triggered, see it as an opportunity to heal, learn, and grow. Being triggered is entirely different than being abused; no one should ever stay in an abusive relationship. If that person triggers you, something inside of you is dying to be healed and let out; you will do the same to him. Work with someone—someone who will point out where you are both going wrong and re-route, keep stepping in the direction to activate each other's badassery, vs. triggering each other. You will get better at recognizing when you and your partner are triggered and at stopping it before it turns into an all-out battle that no one wins.

You can absolutely step into your masculine in all areas of your life, fine-tuning the balance as you notice what is working and what needs more of your powerful, life-giving, womb-magic feminine energy.

The Trail Ride

Ok, back to the actual story. Gracie and I were going to drive to my parents' for a week while Scott went on a business trip. It had been lovely winter days while visiting my parents, and my mom suggested that she and I go on a trail ride with their horses. "Sure," I said. We scheduled it and went. It was later in the afternoon, and we left when Gracie was napping so grandpa could take care of her when she woke up. The trail was beautiful, and we were having a great time.

I hadn't been on a horse for many years at this point, but had spent my butt in the saddle multiple days a week for most of my childhood and teens, so it felt like riding a bike. This horse was new to my parents and hadn't been ridden for a while. I didn't know him, but he seemed to be a docile guy, so I chose him over my old, somewhat higher-energy mare. It had been years, and I wanted it to feel comfortable.

As we were walking down the trail, I sensed he kept trying to walk into the bushes and trees, even though he wasn't gimping or showing any signs of discomfort. I was starting to gather that he wanted me off, but I kept going. The walk turned into asking for a trot, and that was all he needed to prove that my intuition was correct. He started bucking, not a little buck, a large buck, and my "rusty in the saddle" butt came right out. I wasn't expecting it, and looking back, I wasn't riding for it. Out I came, and straight down on my left shoulder and neck, I landed—pretty much one of the worst places to land.

The Accident and Recovery

I won't get into the whole story as that would take too long. However, we were up on a mountain that paramedics had to hike up and carry me out.

My father had to meet us there to take the horses home, so my mom could go to the hospital with me, and while I was being wheeled into the ambulance, all I saw were those tiny little 14-month-old eyeballs looking back at me. I was terrified. I was in a lot of pain, multiple thoughts were racing through my head, the main ones being about this little soul I needed to raise, and the other on if my toes were moving. "I am pretty sure that was a good sign that I would walk again," I kept thinking.

I had a broken clavicle and severely bruised ribs. Still, mainly, I had fear locked into my body and brain. They had to keep me overnight since I was still on blood thinners and was in a lot of pain with my body hitting the ground so hard. I have a pretty high pain tolerance; my pain was a sign my body wasn't happy with what had happened. I was frozen by the thought of not being the best possible mom I could be for Gracie.

Scott was on the next flight from Canada and barely slept. He was there in the wee hours of the hospital room, checking on me.

The Clarity That Came

Over the next few weeks of recovery, I didn't think about my worth in terms of income-generating jobs. I didn't think about whether I was contributing enough to be an acceptable wife, citizen, and woman in this dog-eat-dog world. I didn't think about all the ways I needed to prove myself in every possible way to tell family, friends, and the world around me that I was enough—enough for just staying at home with this precious soul who needed her mom.

I was enough—enough to nurture my home, my husband, and this precious gift from God. I was living in a sliver of time; this season of young motherhood would pass quickly, and now I wanted to soak in every moment of it. I wanted to have no regrets looking back because I was on the teeter-totter women get placed on the moment they even consider trying to get pregnant. In those hospital moments, contemplating all these thoughts, I was shattering through the beliefs and glass ceiling about what a mother should perform like. I was raising the floor on what would now be my new standards for the life I was living.

Days after, I was recovering, still in pain, managing my blood thinners. I catapulted into a new reality, seeing myself as a powerhouse fighting the good fight to stay home and personally raise this impressionable human. I will never shame moms for going back to work. I was the product of a working mom, and I functioned really well with her example, but I didn't want to repeat it.

Over the next few weeks, I had a lot of time to listen to all the thoughts that came in, the ones that liked to bully me into thinking I wasn't enough. The world and the judgment of certain family members started to shrink because nothing mattered more than taking care of that little girl and creating an environment with as few regrets as possible. I couldn't stand the thought of her graduating and me thinking I should've, could've, would've. Now listen, we are imperfect humans raising imperfect children; there is going to be some of that, but it won't be because I couldn't choose a side on the damn teeter-totter!

Back to That Green Couch

Several months later, after seeing a chiropractor for my shaken-up back and finally feeling a bit back to normal, minus the exhaustion, I decided to see a naturopath, who proceeded to tell me I had adrenal fatigue. Through our conversations, she led me to the lady in her office to process the horse accident through EMDR. This was a pivotal moment in my life, sitting on that green couch, looking at her as if she were talking about something so foreign and unrealistic to me. This conversation would be a pivotal snowball that would set me on a new path in my life.

The Lesson

Don't subscribe to the collective of what a woman "should" be; we are everything at once. The world is loud; it is hard to hear yourself, especially if you are a people pleaser. There will always be someone who disagrees with your path as a woman or mom. What matters is that you are genuinely aligned with your gut and are doing what is right for your family, children, and you!

All women will want something different, and that is not wrong; it's perfectly aligned with their soul's path as long as they feel it deep in their gut and womb, not the pressure of society.

Reflection Questions

The world will always have an opinion about what you should do as a woman and mother. Your only job is to listen to your own inner knowing.

1. **Where in your life have you done something you regretted as a mother or woman because the collective told you that is what women do?** How would you like to change that moving forward?

2. **Where might you need to go back in and give yourself empathy for something you harbor and have sadness around?** Every mom will have her regrets. What is something you can forgive yourself for that you now realize is all you knew in the moment?

3. **Where are you running in your wounded masculine—pushing, commanding, white-knuckling your way through life?** What would it feel like to move through your day in pleasure and flow instead?

CHAPTER 27
SNEAKY PRAISE

This was the chapter where I learned that the people-pleaser could be manipulated through compliments—and I finally saw the trap.

Praise had always been my weakness. Tell me I'm doing a good job, and I'll work twice as hard. The people-pleaser lived for recognition. And people who understood that? They knew exactly how to play me.

Until I caught them.

So there I sat on the green couch while this woman helped me process the horse accident and the energy I carried around it out of my body through the help of EMDR, which I totally recommend; it's a wild process. This was an essential step because I had developed adrenal fatigue. With that, we needed to get my adrenaline and cortisol to get back into a less stressed mode, as it was constantly on edge, draining my hormones. The naturopath was working on my nutrition and supplements, and she referred me to process the grief out of my body, knowing that was an essential part in lowering my stress hormones and helping me heal.

As I sat on the couch, she said, "Just because they are family doesn't mean you have to be around them," again staring at her as though she was trying to explain gravity to an alien. For some of you, this may not be your type of people pleaser, but it was mine. Family is important. Again, even if you really didn't get along, disagreed, and didn't necessarily want to be around each other, I witnessed that you still gathered, even if you avoided each other. This doctor was blowing my mind.

We bantered back and forth as I asked her curious questions about this foreign land she was speaking of. She changed my paradigm that day as we discussed how this would apply to the relationships in my life that needed boundaries. I left her office feeling lighter, like the lock from my shackles had been opened, and I could choose if I took them off or not. I didn't know how to take them off, but the fact that I could see that they had been opened was a massive shift for me.

I was only able to test one relationship with this theory over the next year, and I didn't see that person often. This time, when I invited other family members to a gathering, I didn't invite her. She frequently misunderstood me and lacked boundaries. I always walked away feeling bad about myself, yet I didn't have any boundaries either, so I was also playing my role. I wouldn't be able to tell her the ways she hurt me, nor did I think that was necessary per that specific situation, but creating a safe zone where I didn't have to have her around was growth enough.

Preschool and the Decision About More Children

During this time, Gracie was preschool age, and we had found a preschool that I felt really comfortable with, in my overprotective heart. It was all locked down, like a tiny preschool prison, with strict security at check-in. They had a rigorous yet fun schedule for preschoolers, and took their jobs teaching these little ones seriously. We decided it would be good for Gracie to go to preschool two days a week to provide her with a different environment and to be around kids her age.

Gracie is an only child. I ended up having to get a stent placed in my hip because the blood clots never conformed. I spoke with my hematologist when Gracie was about two years old, and when we looked at my history of events with the blood thinners, most of the 10% of reactions that could happen happened with me. After a very long and serious discussion, we decided it wouldn't be safe for me to have another baby. I wasn't expecting this news, so I had to grieve knowing that part of my life was done. I had to grieve that I wouldn't get to relive a baby's first few months of life in a less scared, already-been-there-done-that kind of way.

On the other hand, I wasn't about to risk my life to give Gracie a sibling when, in my mind, she needed a mom more. When I say risk my life, it isn't about the pregnancy; it was about the blood thinners and Lovenox. I was told that I would have to be on them for a short time if getting pregnant, and a tiny percentage of people can have reactions that create deadly clots. So when we looked at our options of me carrying again, it didn't make sense. It didn't make sense to hire a surrogate or even adopt. We threw around those ideas for a couple of years, with Scott and me never being on the same page at the same time. It was meant to be that Gracie would be our only child, and the joy radiating from us at having one healthy, happy child was enough for both of us.

Up until she was about seven, people would ask me if we were going to have more kids. I would say "no, she will be an only child." People would look at me as though I had three heads. I just got used to humorously and sarcastically saying, "Yes, I am going to make her the worst child ever." There is a stereotype of "spoiled only kids," yet I truly believe Gracie was sent here to defy it, because people approach me all the time to tell me how kind and awesome she is. She fulfilled something in both my husband and me with her soul. She is wonderful, delightful, confident, respectful, beautiful, creative, and so, so kind. I know plenty of people whose children have siblings, and those kids are more "spoiled" than Gracie. It is all in how you raise them, and also, I believe, it has to do with what their souls came here to be.

The Part-Time Job

Although enrolling her in school was to prepare her for kindergarten, and also to let her make new friends, I found my next adventure. My husband needed to have some blood work done and check in on a few health concerns. A few miles away was a natural clinic that hosted a Chiropractic Internist in a tiny farm town, so he went there for an appointment. We had moved on to another piece of property after fixing up our first house. This new property had 2.5 acres and potential for a horse. He went to his appointment and was chit-chatting with the doctor who ran and owned the place. The doctor jokingly said, "If you know of any good MAs, let me know." My husband replied, "My wife." It was meant to be. Scott asked if I wanted to work part-time while Gracie was in school, and I was curious, so I went to the interview in this Internist's office and was offered the job. It was five minutes from our house, and they knew it would only be days I didn't have Gracie. It was perfect. I would get that adult talking time, use my skills, and still be there for Gracie.

Praise as Manipulation

It went really well for a year. Gracie was doing pretty well, adjusting to life, and I was getting to assist with natural medicine. The primary doctor figured out how to work my people-pleasing ways by complimenting my work and pace; therefore, I took it as "I should work even harder." Oh boy, here it came. My worth was in my work again. This beast was complicated to slay. Of course, everyone wants to do a good job and be well-received, but I took it to the next level. Those compliments were like adding fuel to an already large fire. It didn't need to be bigger.

He was good. I'll give him that

.

The compliments came first—praise for my work, my pace, my value. And then, smooth as silk, they ask: Can you add another day?

The old me was already calculating. How could I make it work? How could I twist my schedule to accommodate his request? The people-pleaser was salivating at the recognition.

But something was different now. A small voice—the new me—was watching. Noting. Suspicious.

Although I had been shifting out of people-pleasing mode, this one was sneaky and made me reluctant to let the doctors down. It was a full-circle moment when I was chatting with my mom on the phone about the kudos he threw my way, and then, ever so slightly and smoothly, asked for more. I didn't even see it until my mom called it out on the phone: "He buttered you up first, then asked."

The spell broke.

The people-pleaser had been played—and for the first time, I saw the game clearly. Compliment, then request. Praise, then ask for more. It was a formula, and I had been falling for it my entire life.

But not anymore. The woman who needed praise to function? She was dying. And in her place was someone who could see the strings.

But I didn't loop for days on how I could still make it work or how I would feel bad for not giving more of myself to please the other person; I was healing. The looping thoughts were dying.

I thought it was beautiful how my mom, the workaholic, pointed this out and advised me not to fall into that trap. I went back and told him no.

No apology. No lengthy explanation. No scrambling to soften the blow. Just: No.

The people-pleaser inside me flinched, waiting for the fallout. But I didn't waver. I was the mom who chose to be there for Gracie—and no amount of praise was going to manipulate me out of that.

This was the beginning of a new me—one who could smell the trap and walk the other way.

Choosing Gracie

I would have to prove that, in the upcoming months, when Gracie was starting to be bitten, shoved, and hit at this preschool, and because the offending child's parents were major supporters of this private school, nothing would be done to correct that child's behavior. I gave my notice at work, pulled Gracie out of preschool, and started homeschooling her. It's one thing to show up knowing there isn't tolerance for this behavior and keep working through it, but it's another when it isn't acknowledged and corrected.

Some family members were slightly concerned that I wouldn't put her back into another preschool, but my heart sang so loudly that I was the best person to show this girl what the world is like, so we did it at home, while enjoying time with friends who didn't hurt. In time, we were shown an even bigger path that God was priming us for. He always knows our plans before we do.

The Property Search

We had been on the two and a half acres for about two years, enough to have just finished all our updates and overhauls, working nonstop on weekends and some evenings. It was a cozy, cottagey-style home, with a beautiful wooden three-rail fence, a gorgeous sunroom, and an arena we had just created for our new horses. Gracie was about to turn five, and we felt pretty good about life, but didn't have a deep sense of being settled in this home. I love the property and home we created, but an HOA controlled the neighborhood, and it was somewhat close to a main highway, which made for some road noise. The people who know my husband know he does not belong in an HOA. I learned that he doesn't belong in the city when at our first home, he was in the backyard with a tractor tilling up the old grass to plant new grass and creating a dust bowl for the neighbors. I felt like the rednecks of the neighborhood. We didn't belong in the city, but we gave it a good run!

We finally just had the house painted the color I wanted after we fixed everything on the house and the land. Two months after finally having the house in the color I desired, we saw God's plan for us to move again, this time to a home we hoped to settle in. Since I left and moved to California, this would be the 9th time I've packed up the whole house and moved within 12 years. It was time we settled, and God had just the spot.

We decided, in the fall—fall seems to be life-shifting for us—that I would go down and spend a week with my parents, bringing Gracie to see them. They still came up about every two months to see us—mainly her. We had talked for the past year about them buying a condo near where we live so that they could spend half the year at home and the other half around Gracie. It was so hard when they left. I missed them and could mainly hold it together, but now this little 4-year-old would look out the window, waving and crying as they drove away. She loves her grandparents, and it was torture when they left.

We didn't get as many opportunities to spend a week at their house, so we decided to stay for a couple of weeks this time. My husband now works from home with the same company and decided to tag along, bringing work with him. Our good friends, whom we had gotten close with in the first neighborhood, wanted to go camping in that area with their kids, so we had big plans to meet up with them and camp as well. It was a fantastic couple of weeks filled with outdoor time in the mountains and a lot of laughing.

The Evening Walk

My parents still lived in the beautiful house they built when I was growing up, down a picturesque country road. My mom and I enjoyed going for long walks and talking while Gracie played with Grandpa. It was the eve of our last day before we headed home, and I asked my mom to go for a walk. We typically walked about 2.5 miles and turned around, making it a nice, long, enjoyable time. This town is nestled in the mountains, with small rolling hills and valleys, creating a beautiful scenery and a tapestry everywhere you look. Every time my husband and I traveled back, it was like seeing it for the first time again. We got so used to city scenery that we forgot how beautiful it was at home. It's a small mountain town, and it didn't offer much work in my husband's industry. As much as we wanted grandparents to be closer, his job was more important. He had worked so hard and was now finishing his master's degree.

We were enjoying the crisp fall air. The mountains to our west were glowing in reds and oranges, showing the last bit of daylight, and the smell of sweet, moist grass from the last cut of hay the farmers were bailing was enticing my nose. On this walk, we couldn't help but reminisce about the reality that tomorrow was the last day before we headed home, and how quickly two weeks had gone by. A flash of light on a ridge across the valley below caught my eye. It was where one of our previous school teachers lived. In fact, a few of our teachers lived down that lane, which had a couple of houses on a ridge, each of them dipping down into beautiful, spacious pastures. I said, "I wouldn't mind living where Mrs. Lake lives," referencing the teacher who lived in a charming old farmhouse. We both sighed at wishful thinking and changed the subject.

The Discovery

It was dark, and we could see the shop light on as we walked up the driveway. Scott and my dad were out tinkering on some of his latest woodworking projects and confirmed that Gracie had gone to bed. I walked into the house quietly, shutting the slamming screen door, tiptoeing up the stairs, and I fell onto the guest bed in the dark blue and grey room. A thought popped into my mind, "What properties are available in this town right now?" Scott and I had become attached to thinking about and looking up real estate. We always liked to see what the market was doing, and if there was a new place to buy and fix up, it became addictive to search for. At one point, we considered moving to Texas to get closer to his work, but it never really aligned with our desires. We made that disappointing "pros and cons" list my mother has success with and ended up, again, with our hands tied and my internal decision to never make the list again. That is when I really started to form a deeper connection with my intuition, rather than relying on paper.

"What is available here in this tiny little town?" As I entered the specs and clicked the search button, my heart beat faster. A house on "teacher lane" was listed. I looked at what it had to offer. It was dated, but the main things were there: land, a one-story house, and a barn for the horses. There were two things I told my husband I couldn't imagine living without now that we have them in our current home. I didn't know how I would give up my sunroom windows or the charming three-rail fencing I had come to love. I emailed the listing realtor and asked if we could see the property the next day, showered, and went to bed.

Was it wrong for me to flirt with the idea that there could be a house within a few minutes of where I grew up? Flirt with the idea that we could move here, or would want to move back to the town we grew up in? Perhaps, but there was only one way to find out. I asked Scott to go with me the next day while my parents stayed with Gracie. He, too, was curious because this was a little game our brains liked to play, and although we both knew most likely his job wouldn't allow him to move to this small town with a tiny airport, we both thought, "What is the harm in looking?" My parents didn't get their hopes up because we had talked about this before and had driven by other houses on other trips, just to drive them and ourselves crazy, knowing it wouldn't happen, but curiosity got the best of us. They thought, yeah, yeah, go, get it out of your system.

The Perfect Property

We did. The house and property were rough, but they had great bones and potential. Someone had just come in and repainted the inside yellow and installed new flooring and lighting throughout the house, a significant expense that is now out of the way. However, the house needed a ton of updating, a conversion to create an office, and the acreage needed everything: fences, irrigation management, and clearing of overgrown vegetation, as it had been left alone for years. There were random things everywhere, and no functioning system was running anything.

When you walked in the front door, you forgot all the work that needed to be done. The view greeted you with welcoming arms through an entire wall of windows facing the mountains. My breath was taken away. It wouldn't have a sunroom, but the amount of light in this place and the enormous windows made the entire house light up. Looking out toward those mountains, I realized there was one three-rail fence on the place separating the yard from the pasture near the house. I couldn't believe what was happening, the fact that we saw this severely run-down house and land as desirable. We had now flipped two houses and knew the transformation that could occur with some hard work, but this was a lot more acreage and a lot more work.

I was so in awe. It checked the box for a few things my husband was picky about, and for the two things I didn't think I could live without. Was it God's direction? Was this where we were to move? We drove home the next day, scheming in the truck that we wouldn't tell my parents we were now planning to surprise them and flip our third property.

The Lesson

I didn't realize how sneaky praise was still manipulating me. The people-pleasing "performer" decided to try again to see if I would bite. Until that point, I didn't realize how persuaded I was by recognition and affirmation. It was all from a deep sense of being seen, and to a people pleaser, it was my love language. "You compliment me, I'll double my work." When I felt seen and was told I did well, I felt accepted and needed, and who doesn't want that?

I really believe it was a God moment for my mom to recognize and protect my journey as a mother, since she had lived and seen a different path. She could've easily encouraged me to do the same. I could've still said yes, I could've worked more. It could've been a tricky situation, but it wasn't when my daughter needed me. I dropped everything and was able to help her, returning to what I was meant to do during this period of my life: be her number one support and guidance, choosing the path I was meant to be on instead of helping an office that was outside my desires.

Reflection Questions

Praise can be a powerful tool for manipulation when you're a people pleaser who craves validation.

1. **Do you find that you only feel good about yourself when you receive affirmations from others?** What do you notice yourself doing when others compliment you? Do you work harder, or do you receive the compliment and continue on your way?

2. **Are you someone who seeks compliments, waiting for others to recognize the work you do?** How does it feel in your body when they don't speak it?

3. **Can you think of a time when someone praised you and then immediately asked for more?** How did you respond? What will you do if you are in that situation?

Untamed Bonus

I feel a deep mothering energy wash over me when I see women not stepping into their power. I had deep concerns about whether I would be capable as a mother before I had Gracie. I doubted myself and wondered if I was qualified to uphold such an important role. Even though we were a stable married couple who didn't do drugs or drink much alcohol, we didn't enjoy going out to late-night parties; we loved staying home, and we had so much love and a caring family surrounding us.

I am no longer working out those insecurities about what motherhood requires and looks like. I sometimes wonder if my soul beckoned to be named Rachel, "motherly," calling forth the desire to nurture you deeply. I see you, I acknowledge you, and call you back into who you are meant to be. I want to help you recognize the learned behaviors that no longer serve you and guide you in identifying how you are destroying yourself, playing small, and feeling incapable.

I wasn't meant to have multiple children come from my womb; I was meant to hold you in a powerful, dark, and light feminine space, reminding you to spread your wings and fly.

Blissful Bonus Questions

Take a moment to sit with these deeper questions. Let yourself feel held in this mothering energy.

1. **What have you done to feel validated?** Have you felt held, loved, and seen by the "mother" energy in your life? How does she show up for you?

2. It might even be a grandma or an older friend who contains this sacred energy in your life. **Is there anything you need to forgive her for?**

3. **Can you see how she did the absolute best she could, even if you would've wanted something slightly different?**

4. **Do you have children?** Are you repeating things you don't desire to come into play?

5. **How can you show the motherly energy for yourself at this time?** What memory can you recall and offer that little girl love, support, and nourishment you didn't receive in that moment?

CHAPTER 28
SHUT THE DAMN DOOR

This chapter is about what happens when you leave doors cracked open—and the monsters that chase you through them.

The people-pleaser loves to leave doors open. "Maybe they'll change." "Maybe I'm being too harsh." "Maybe I should give them another chance."

But I was learning: some doors need to be slammed shut, locked, and walked away from. Forever.

The Secret Plan

It was happening. We were under contract, and the inspection was scheduled for a week later. We still hadn't told anyone—not my family, not Scott's, and not even Gracie, although I had started packing our home slowly and putting the boxes where she wouldn't see them. We told our family we would come down to visit them and celebrate Gracie's 5th birthday with them instead of hosting my usual large party. The day after her party would be the inspection, and we would be able to spend time on the property, exploring and dreaming of all we desired to fix.

Everything was in order. Scott's stay-at-home job didn't care if he moved, and we had our current home under contract. I couldn't believe this was happening. We were moving back to our hometown after thirteen years away. We had spread our wings and flown, and now we were headed back to a place that felt so familiar, yet I was also starting to realize how uncomfortable it felt. Remember, it was a small town, and I left friends and a previous boyfriend whose relationships didn't end the way my heart had hoped. People talk, and talk is cheap, but in a small town, many people get caught up in listening. The gossip circles can run strong in a small town.

Reaching Out to Old Friends

I reached out to my former friend group to let them know I would be moving back. A few years prior, we had all gotten together for a near-10-year post-graduation reunion. I had the thought now that I was moving back, we could create new friendships with our now-older, wiser, and more worldly adventures under our belts. However, not all of them left; instead, they made the same pattern of grown-up-mom cliques with the people who stayed. There would be no support or excitement from them about me moving back; it was short, to-the-point "great."

I was a bit shocked, given we had an adult slumber party and reconnected, but I soon realized I was relieved and thankful they didn't give me more. God had other plans—plans for other, deeper, more connected, and supportive friends who were about to enter my life. I wasn't and still won't fall into the petty gossip and behavior of high school drama; I left long ago. Like a little kid, getting her hand slapped in the cookie jar, God slapped mine. That was the last time I would ever try to connect with any of them, and it's been magical ever since, knowing my boundary.

I saw one of them once, and she acted like we were best friends again. She went in for a hug in front of others, as if she were performing in a play, but I shifted and repositioned gently, offering her a smile and a "good to see you." Fakeness is one of my least favorite qualities in people. My husband can spot it a mile away and doesn't put up with any of it. He has been a pillar in reminding me who I am and in redirecting me to pull up my bootstraps and straighten my crown. Again, hi, "eternal optimist here," thinking everyone has the best intentions. Note to self: they don't.

Facing What We Left Behind

The build-up to this move was like my heart being broken wide open and displayed for all to see. We both could feel the deep pull and desire to go back, that it was the right thing to do for Gracie and the life we wanted to live, but we had to face what we had left behind. Neither of us left anything on bad terms; we just left with hard things unfolding in our lives.

He didn't get to explore our town much as a kid; his dad was strict, and he was at basketball, school, working on the farm, and, as a hobby, working on cars. That was it. There were no fun, family, joyous activities that sparked his interest and happiness. Just as he was leaving for the Marine Corps, his parents told him they would be divorcing, and his childhood home was sold while he was gone. He was a stranger to the town he grew up in, and I felt like I was the friend wearing a scarlet A on my chest coming home.

We didn't focus on that for long because we had a surprise in mind for my parents. Remember, we like to surprise them in person, and this would be a doozy.

The Big Reveal

We arrived the day before the inspection. I played it off the next morning casually as Scott came up from a business call. "Hey, babe, that one house is still on the market from five weeks ago. Want to go again and see if we have any different thoughts about it?" He casually responded, "Sure." I looked at my parents, who I knew didn't have anything to do that day because we were in town, and asked if they would like to join us, as they also liked home projects. They said yes and wondered why we would waste our time getting our hopes up when Scott couldn't ever get a job here.

We all went, Gracie in tow. It was as rough as we left it, though it was soon to be ours, and we were wearing rose-colored glasses when we attempted to gauge the magnitude of the work it would require. We walked into the front door and meandered through to the garage. We wanted to convert the garage into an office, a second living room, and a guest room because we needed a little more space. I casually asked my dad if he thought we could convert something like this. He had worked for an electric company for years, was a woodworker, and they had built their house, so we were trying to play it off. He was mystified and paused, wondering why we would go to such lengths, but he amused us because, as I said, we were always talking about real estate.

He looked around and said, "Yeah, I think you could easily convert this garage." My mom was deflated because, a few minutes earlier, our realtor had said out loud that the property was now "under contract," which made my heart nearly leap out of my throat, thinking she had just ruined our surprise. Turns out it worked in our favor because my mom assumed it was under contract with someone else. Her mind was spinning with thoughts of, "let's not torture ourselves, it's already spoken for," so I let it out. "Yeah, that is too bad, it's already under contract; however, I'm glad you think it is possible to convert the garage, because we are the ones on the contract."

The brief millisecond of silence turned into my mom's face dropping into her hands and a deep, sorrowful wail coming from this petite woman. My dad started to tear up as we heard a cheery and questionable "really." It was epic. My mom couldn't breathe. There was nothing in the house except for one roll of toilet paper, which she went, pulled off the holder, and carried around with her for the rest of the four hours we toured the property, sharing our dreams, and the inspector inspected.

It was ours, and we were on our way home.

The Lesson

Taking two steps forward and one step back can be part of the healing process. Just like being in a relationship with someone new will trigger issues from past relationships. It had been years since I'd seen these girls, and somehow stepping back into a space where I had spent most of my time with them made the "loyal" people pleaser show up, enticing something I thought I wanted. I wasn't close with them when I moved away. We had barely been in touch, yet the hope of the "what if" appeared after a fun girls' night out reconnecting, and that door had slightly cracked open for me to desire looking again into something familiar. This was the work of the cortex, the part of the brain that likes to keep you safe and in situations that are similar and familiar.

I had to shut the damn door, lock it, and throw away the key

It felt as though I had taken ten million steps forward into the next chapter of friendships. I know it was a piece of the healing process, a piece where they didn't choose me, but where, in the end, I would never choose those friendships again, and that is a powerful place to be.

What door are you leaving cracked open, hoping someone else will close it for you?

Slam it. Lock it. Walk away.

The people-pleaser will tell you that's harsh, that you should give more chances, that maybe they'll change. But the woman who is breaking free? She knows: some doors protect you. And closing them isn't cold—it's claiming your peace.

Reflection Questions

Sometimes the most loving thing we can do is shut the door on relationships that no longer serve us.

1. **Do you have a door open in a relationship that you have forgotten to close, lock, and throw away the key?** Who is it?

2. **Why do you let them back in?** What about them is so great that you can't find it on your own?

3. **Are you staying in relationships because they are familiar?**

4. **What quality do you need to fulfill within yourself to stop seeking those old relationships?**

CHAPTER 29
BECOMING THE BLACK SHEEP

I moved back to the place I came from—but I was not the same woman who had left.

Everyone expected me to slide right back into the old traditions, the old dynamics, the old role. Agreeable Rachel. Accommodating Rachel. Rachel, who never rocked the boat.

They were about to meet someone new. Someone who had learned that rocking the boat doesn't sink it—it just takes it in a new direction.

The Move and The Mess

We had moved, and a caravan of family helped us again. Our belongings had filled a three-story house, a garden shed, a full garage, and a barn. Additionally, we now had horses, cats, and dogs. It was a lot, but I was a pro at packing and organizing what we would need when we got there and even had the paint and all the tools out and ready to start painting, ripping out trim, converting the garage, ripping out a bathtub in Gracie's bathroom, and replacing all the windows within the first couple of weeks of moving in. We always set up our beds first so we could get good sleep, but the rest of the house was a war zone. Luckily, we now live close to where we grew up, on adjoining county roads five minutes apart. It was close—so close—that we stayed with my parents for the first few nights while we made a mess in the new house. We were nuts, and we had the home improvement bug—a nasty one. It was so addictive for both of us to watch a home come back to life.

The entire inside of the house was a soft yellow, which was entirely outside my wheelhouse of décor, so my mom and I started painting every single room. Gracie's room would be repainted blue with floating clouds, as I had just done in her previous room two months before we moved. We were tired, wired, and full of excitement. We felt like it was familiar and all new at the same time. We noticed that living in the country was a real treat because it made driving anywhere easy. If it said you would get there in thirty minutes, you would. There wasn't a massive amount of traffic, and any increase barely slowed us down.

Old Traditions, New Questions

We moved to this new house a week before Thanksgiving, and we were thrown back into the traditions I was raised with, seeing the same family members for Thanksgiving and Christmas, even if we didn't desire to—not that we didn't like them, we had just become so accustomed to starting new traditions. It was a tradition that my mom and her brothers created when my brother and I, along with about ten cousins, were growing up. Back then, it was fun. Now, most of the cousins had moved away. My aunts and mom were still rotating houses, with each hosting one of the main holidays, and no one questioned whether it still actually worked.

But I was back, and had a newfound sense of permission from my EMDR doctor to rock the boat—not that I needed permission, but that is what I felt I received that day, sitting in her office. We got through the first year of all the holidays, also hosting some of Scott's family while we were still moving in. It was a mess and felt like complete chaos in our new home. However, Scott and I were trying to embrace all the new situations around us. We had been our own family and couple for so long, and suddenly, we were thrown into a big, loving family that was also trying to find a new path, and it was a bit bumpy.

The first year of holidays was fun and reminiscent of what used to be, yet it also had me pondering whether it was the tradition I wanted to move forward with. As the early months of the new year buzzed by, we found ourselves tired after months of working weekends and weeknights in our new home. Early spring was upon us, and outdoor activities were amping up. The thought crossed my mind a few times, "Oh my heavens, what did we do? Did we make the right choice?" We worked too much, yet we can't seem to stop because of the satisfaction of watching this property come back to life. Thank heavens we had so much help from my dad and my brother—they helped us get the momentum going in our new place. My dad practically led the remodel inside, and my brother was always over helping where he could, inside and out. It was truly a gift!

I couldn't deny the fact that we had started enjoying a few more evenings of cocktails to get through this stressful yet satisfying time. We were becoming aware of new boundaries with family and with each other. It took us a couple of years of working nonstop on this property to find a better balance between work, play, and family time, and to alleviate the unnecessary pressure on my marriage that had arisen because we were both so tired.

Rocking the Boat

I remember being the boat rocker that next fall, when we had almost lived in our new home for a year. I didn't want to travel to other people's homes for Thanksgiving and Christmas. I didn't want to slip right into all the old traditions, as if I'd never left and was a kid again. I had a kid, a husband, and a full-fledged life of decisions that would or wouldn't work for my family, no matter how insane they sounded to people outside our home.

So I struck the match.

I told my mom: We're not going anywhere for Christmas. We're not hosting. This year, we stayed home—just us.

The people-pleaser braced for impact. She expected tears, guilt trips, and the silent treatment. She expected to be labeled selfish, talked about at family dinners, and cast out.

My mom was shocked. But she didn't crumble. And neither did I.

I had rocked the boat—and it didn't sink. It just took a new direction.
 I was much more independent than I had been when I left, and she respected my ideas and my family's wishes. She agreed it might be nice to break that tradition and only continue with the whole family for Thanksgiving. So I sent out the text, and instead of getting a lot of resistance, it was met with open arms.

Here's what I learned: People will stay trapped in traditions that no longer serve them for DECADES, just to avoid a single uncomfortable conversation.

The people-pleaser loves tradition—because tradition doesn't require courage. It only requires compliance.

But the woman becoming untamed? She asks: Does this still serve me? Does this feed my soul or drain it? And if the answer is drain—she changes it. Even if people are shocked. Even if they whisper. Even if she becomes the black sheep.

The black sheep isn't the shame of the family. She's the one brave enough to live differently.

I love tradition, yet not all traditions need to move forward or serve as they once did. It's okay to rock the boat if your heart is sending off rocket ships of desire. Follow them, see what happens.

That year was the first of many Christmases when we would spend hours opening gifts, watching each person unwrap a gift, making each moment heartfelt and special, rather than rushing through gifts to clean, get ready to host others, or hurry out the door to attend someone else's Christmas dinner. We invite our immediate family over, have them stay the night, and spend the whole day in comfy clothes, listening to Christmas music, and watching the snow fall, as if we're in our own snow globe, with the world shut down in a peaceful celebration. I shut the door entirely on what was no longer serving my family and never looked back, knowing these were the traditions I wanted to create.

The Boss Babe Who Ran

Onto another story about asking for what you desire—a few days ago, I received a text from an old friend who is 10 years older than me. I met her right out of high school; she was a boss in her job at the time. Her life was bumping and grinding toward the direction she wanted, and even when she stayed at home with her kids, she chose to build a home-based career and was crushing it. She was a boss babe.

At home, however, she had a husband she wasn't happy with. I watched over the years as her slight unhappiness turned into frustration, disconnection, and, eventually, disdain, leading the two of them to live separate lives under the same roof for the next fifteen years. Ten years ago, she ended up getting thyroid cancer and beat it, but it changed her, as it would anyone. She couldn't see a way out with her husband. She had never alluded to the fact that after twenty years of marriage, he was physically abusive in any way, but it was as though she was running, running from facing him and requesting a divorce. I am not an advocate for divorce, but in some situations, it is the reality that needs to be addressed.

She had a problem with alcohol during a difficult few years while coming out of her cancer scare. Her goal was to remain married to her husband until all her children went to college. My loves, what are you teaching your children as they witness such unhappiness, discontent, and hatred in a home? How will they view their own marriages in the future, and what possibilities will be available to them? I would listen to her—the few times we saw each other over the past ten years—and empathize, energizing her, allowing her to remember who she was and reclaim her power. She stopped using alcohol, not per my influence but the children staring back at her, yet she was still living a life of avoidance, a life of fear of approaching this man for a divorce.

The text I received and the conversation I had brought tears to my eyes. Instead of facing this man in court over a divorce, she bought a camper a few years ago and went from craft show to craft show selling her goods. Again, a brilliant businesswoman. Soon, her car broke down, she parked the camper at her parents' house, and lived out of it. Although she didn't admit it, my heart tells me substances became involved. I can't 100% confirm that; however, she has supportive, amazing parents who are no longer talking to her and have kicked her off their property. She decided to walk away from a gorgeous house her dad helped her and her husband build on a slice of her parents' property, and is now homeless.

Yes, homeless, living with some guy in a tent, and hadn't showered in weeks. My heart sank. Who was this person? Was I speaking with the same strong, independent, fearless woman who says everything she thinks without hesitation, who was a very natural businesswoman, and now cannot take a shower, buy food, or drive a car to where she wants to go? It was beyond shocking.

I offered her the help I could while also trying to call her back into her power, reminding her that she has a home, can get a lawyer, and can divorce her husband to secure her assets and get back on her feet. But she didn't want to, she couldn't imagine taking those steps, so instead of closing the door on her nearly thirty-year marriage, which I have heard about her unhappiness for 25 of those years, she ran. She left the door wide open and allowed the monster on the other side to chase her, chase her into a life that isn't even recognizable, chase her into most likely using alcohol and possibly drugs. I was baffled. She wasn't herself. It was as if, instead of facing the giant of her husband and being backed by so many people in her corner, she turned to what she thought was easier.

My loves, maybe you cannot relate to this story, as most of us would clean bathrooms at the worst gas station to claim a room over our heads, but can you relate to running from something? Something you haven't faced, the dark hole staring back at you through that open door? Have you told the darkness how it needed to change, and then you've closed the door, locked it, and thrown away the key, never to return? It might be terrifying, but I would imagine that as hard as she might think it is to face the divorce, it would be easier than living in a leaky tent approaching the winter snow season, wondering where your next meal was coming from, and trying to get a ride to a warmer state so you don't freeze in cold months ahead.

This breaks my heart. I hate to see women drop their crown and forget their own power. She was a badass and an absolute treat to this world. I don't know now where she is or how her future will be written, and that saddens me. It rings even deeper in my soul to tell you, "Pick up that crown, my love, straighten it out, and start fighting for what you desire!"

The Lesson

As a people pleaser, I am sure you want to leave your body when it comes to asking for what you want and desire. It makes you want to run the other direction because the desire seems too big! I knew my husband was a safe place to share my desires, but breaking my family's traditions, which had been in full swing for at least 25 years, felt wrong, selfish, and unapproachable. Until I looked at my reality and thought, "What am I teaching them by not showing up for my personal family's desires?" I would be another follower stepping into the path of doing something because we had "always" done it that way. It was a habit for everyone, not necessarily a desire, that still fit. I knew requesting such a thing would disrupt years of tradition, yet I couldn't unsee what I desired our new traditions to be, and I noticed a new version of me, the version who was willing to shoulder the heavy load of guilt, becoming the black sheep and paving a new path. So I did.

Reflection Questions

Sometimes claiming what we truly desire requires us to be the black sheep, the boat rocker, the one who dares to say "this no longer fits."

1. **What are you running from?** What desire are you avoiding claiming because it would change a tradition that has always been, yet it no longer fits? What makes you afraid of being the black sheep of the family, or dare I say, feeling like the bitch?

2. **What monster is chasing you out of the dark abyss from that door you left wide open?** What are you too afraid to face?

3. **What would happen if you went back and faced the freaking giant?** What would it look like to claim your worth, shut and lock the damn door, and walk away for good?

You aren't here to run—you are here to claim your divine rights. It might feel heavy for a while, but are you willing to stand your ground and expand into the new possibilities waiting for you?

CHAPTER 30
VELVET WHISPERS

This is the chapter where I learned that my worth wasn't tied to my productivity—even when my husband's enormous energy walked into the room.

For years, I couldn't rest without guilt. Couldn't sit for fifteen minutes without feeling like I should be doing something. The people-pleaser had convinced me that stillness was laziness, that my value came from constant motion.

It was time to heal that wound—once and for all.

Exhaustion and Energy

We had been at our new place for almost a year, and had spent every weekend and many weeknights cleaning up the new plot of land God had bestowed upon us. It was exhausting and exhilarating at the same time. I had previously healed from the adrenal fatigue that I had in our prior home. At this new pace, I found myself slipping back into it. I wasn't taking great care of myself. I still cooked from home 90% of the time and love finding healthy, delicious gluten-and dairy-free recipes, but the stress of keeping up a certain pace—my husband's pace—was quickly draining anything I had to give.

He runs at a different pace. Once he sees what needs to be done, he can't find the patience to know that it doesn't have to be done all at once. He had a full-time job, I was busy with Gracie, and we both spent hundreds of hours of any remaining time on DIY projects. Here I was, again wanting to lie on the couch and nap, tired when I got up after sleeping all night, wondering how I was going to put one foot in front of the other that day. This wasn't my normal energy. I am typically a busy bee skipping around the house joyfully getting everything done, yet here I was again with an unrecognizable exhaustion running the show.

Scott has an enormous energy. It's not angry or forceful, but it is piercing. He has a commanding presence in a room, not only because he is big in stature, but also because his energy field is powerful and intense. I have had other men we know approach me in random situations, asking if Scott is mad. I look at them with my head cocked sideways and reply, "No, he's having a great time." It's true, he was having a great time; however, his energy is penetrating, and he can feel big to others who have a hard time regulating him.

Here's what I was finally seeing: I had a wound that activated every time Scott walked into the room, not because of anything he was doing—but because the people-pleaser in me couldn't rest in the presence of productive energy.

I felt like I had to hop to attention, throw the magazine out the window, and prove I had earned the right to sit.

It wasn't his fault. It was mine to heal.

He was mystified, saying, "Babe, I don't care if you look at a magazine, I know you need rest," yet his energy commanded otherwise.

This took me a long time to put into words, but as I healed other parts of my people-pleasing nature, I could see this was one of them. I still had a layer of "production makes me worthy" left inside; it was sneaky and so clever. It caused a few arguments in my marriage as I tried to figure out why he was saying one thing yet showing me another with his energy. His energy felt larger than mine, but my people-pleaser amplified the "worthy if I'm working" wound when he walked into the room. It would make me feel as though I was walking on eggshells to sneak a break for a few minutes, like a little kid sneaking a cookie.

I wanted to blame it on the parent catching me with my hand in the cookie jar and say it was their fault, so I blamed Scott for it being HIS fault and for his energy making me feel a certain way. However, that wasn't true. It was a wound still stuck in the depths of my worthiness, triggered by his enormous energy, and it left me hunched over, feeling judged, unseen, and like a damn mule that always had to work to be loved. There it was again. Once this clicked, he and I had a conversation that finally aligned, and I knew it was another pose I had to hold: the discomfort and breathe into my heart and womb, telling it I was safe and loved, when he walked into the room and saw me enjoying a leisurely moment.

It worked. The trigger is dead.

Now, when Scott walks into the room, and I'm lying on the floor with a magazine, I don't flinch. I don't apologize. I don't scramble to look productive.

I breathe. I stay. I remind myself: I don't have to EARN rest. I am worthy of pleasure without production.

The people-pleaser who tied my worth to my work ethic? She's gone. And in her place is a woman who knows she deserves softness—even on the days she does nothing at all.

The Camping Trip and Divine Download

Around this same time, Scott was traveling again for business, and my parents were traveling about an hour and a half away to a gorgeous mountain town, taking their house on wheels, and going camping. They invited Gracie and me to tag along. She would be starting kindergarten next week, and this would be a great way to wrap up summer. She would attend a shared school where she was taught two days a week in a whole classroom setting, and the books would be sent home with me for the other three days to teach from home. This was the best way to introduce school to her while still allowing me to spend a lot of time raising her.

It was early September, and we were greeted with cold mornings and nights up at 13,000 feet. The back of the camper dropped down and opened to the crisp morning air, where you could catch a glimpse of your breath in front of you. We sat early in the mornings, drinking coffee, wrapped in jammies and blankets. My blanket came with an additional heater in the form of my now-aging dog, Petrie. I had brought my laptop in case I was inspired by anything while I had the great outdoors wrapped around my body. I had always wanted to tell Petrie's life story, and an idea had popped into my mind a few weeks prior that reignited the thought.

My parents wanted to play with Gracie, and I received the urge to open a Word document, so I did. In six hours, I had written six children's emotion books based on Petrie's life. Books based on real-life events from Petrie's life and tied to the complex emotions I imagined her experiencing. I wanted to connect parents back to their kids, allowing them to feel their feelings and to have deeper, sometimes tricky, talks with them. I wanted kids to be seen more—not ignored or misunderstood—and I wanted it to come through in a little dog that loved kids in real life. I wrote them all—truly, with what I believe to be co-creation with the Divine. It poured out of me as though I were the fingers and the Divine the message. I would call them "Petrie's Dish."

I was called back into reality by Gracie giggling and approaching the camper with my parents. I didn't say a thing about the books. I saved it and closed the computer. We enjoyed the last day of camping, exploring the mines and rivers around us. I knew our time with Petrie was getting shorter, and I was so happy she was sitting with me as I recapped some of her significant life events.

The Whispers Begin

A year and a half went by, and I didn't think much about the Petrie stories because I was so busy. I was at a women's Christian retreat for the weekend, enjoying a few nights away and soaking up some luxurious girlfriend time. For the past two years, I had been seeing 11:11 everywhere. It had come to me multiple times a day. It got to be so frequent that I couldn't help it—I looked it up—and thought the answer was pretty intriguing. It was interpreted as a sign of divine guidance and a call to align my thoughts and intuitions to a higher purpose.

Cool, I thought. I hadn't ever been a real "religious" person, but instead "spiritual." I thought it was interesting, contemplated it for a while, and on and off had this faint siren whisper of "helping women." It was so light, yet kept coming over and over for many months. I would hear it, eventually giggling to myself, thinking, "Oh yeah, what am I going to help them with?" Only taking a second to think and then being brought back to the reality of my busy day.

I had fallen into the vortex of YouTube, watching a few accounts I loved: women decorating their homes, posting videos about being a mom, documenting their health journey, and a couple of accounts where I watched women ignite the path for feminine and masculine energies. I didn't have much time. I was a part-time homeschool mom, living on acreage that we were still spending a lot of time working on, and helping support my husband and home in any way necessary. I was busy, but I found time to watch something for a few minutes a day or a week, which was enough to inspire me.

I have always been drawn to outside-the-box self-help books rather than fiction. Although fiction can really pull you in, when I did get a few minutes to myself, I wanted to learn something and be changed by a different way of thinking. It was the divine calling me to my purpose, as the words and videos lit me up. There was a deep stirring in my soul, and I didn't know what to do, so I started a YouTube channel and learned to make and edit videos, which was SO slow because I acted like an eighty-year-old, having avoided social media for a decade.

I didn't want to, yet I kept hearing this whisper to get on. I eventually explored what it would be like and posted some subpar videos, feeling very underqualified and definitely looking like a beginner. I only posted a couple, never really told anyone, and moved on with my busy life.

The Retreat That Changed Everything

It was Gracie's first-grade year, and I kept seeing those numbers and hearing that tug in my heart. I had posted a couple of "cutesy" videos of food, decorating, and some farm stuff, and at the time, I believed that was the purpose of the call. It was February, when I was attending this ladies' Christian retreat about an hour from my house. The ladies at our current church gathered for a weekend of uplifting, powerful connection, with about 60 to 80 of us. We stayed in tiny cabins in the woods, had all-day activities, and devoured delicious food that filled our tummies. Very talented women stood up at the podium, giving a few sermons. The church brought in a female pastor from a few hours away to provide a few talks and enhance the retreat.

That evening, as she started in, I felt an invisible, hot spotlight on me. It was as though every whisper I had heard was coming out of this woman's mouth, tears cascading down my face. Was this really happening? I felt so embarrassed. I had the thought of "why am I crying? There are other women here that we know are suffering from tragedy." They had a purpose for crying; they were going through actual hard times, suffering, and one could understand why they would be moved to tears. But my life was great—fast-paced, worked too much, and tired, but great. There was a veiled feeling that came with the tears, one that weighed so heavily on my chest and kept repeating what it had been saying for the past several months. It was dark and cold outside, and the warmth of the summons and beckoning had me feeling hot.

The pastor asked for the music to begin playing and said that if you needed to be prayed over, come down the aisle and stand by her. Of course, the people who had tragedy strike their lives got up, and others surrounded them, lifting them in prayer. I felt a shove, a nudge to get out of my chair, rise, and have a healing prayer placed over me, so I listened to the voice, and with pure discomfort in my bones, I stood in line feeling self-conscious to be prayed over.

As it was my turn, she just dove right in, didn't ask what I needed, just started pouring light over me. Now the floodgates opened, and I sobbed. I remember a friend who had been through something tragic standing in another circle, looking up at me for a split second. She had a look of confusion in her eyes. We broke the stare of our swelling eyes and returned to our individual rituals. The heaviness lifted, and a lighter, yet exhausted, feeling remained as I exited the room that night and headed back to my cabin. The ceremony was over, and I went to bed.

The next day, I was walking back to my cabin after breakfast when I was caught by that pastor, who asked if I would like to talk about anything bothering me. I replied, "Nothing is bothering me, it's more of a pressure to rise into something I don't feel qualified to do or clear in the direction to go." I told her the message I kept hearing and listed 20 reasons why I didn't feel accredited. She looked at me and replied, "You are being called for a reason. He doesn't make mistakes." Although it was confirming and helpful, I was still reluctant.

COVID and a New Direction

I returned home, and within a week or two, the worldwide COVID-19 pandemic broke out. I started homeschooling my daughter full-time until school was out, and we spent the summer playing with the family at the lake. It was different owning land than living in the city or in an apartment. My heart ached for their confinement. I cannot imagine what many of you went through living in the city. I thought of you often, and how hard it must be to try to contain children, let alone yourself, when you just wanted to get outside and get some fresh air during that scary outbreak.

We had a property where we could go outside and play in nature while the world was in complete confusion and fear. It had been a bizarre summer, even though we had more freedom than most. We were now a week before Gracie's second-grade year was to begin, and had a confusing decision to make. COVID was still in full swing when her school finally decided to move forward with great caution and have the kids back at school. There had been a lot of fear around this outbreak, and I wasn't ready to send my daughter back. Plus, something amazing happened: although she was doing great in school, she excelled for the two months that ended her first-grade year at the beginning of COVID.

We took great care to consider the entire situation and, as a family, made the heartfelt decision that I would homeschool her full-time, something I never thought I would do. I had been trained for the past two years on what a homeschool schedule and curriculum looked like. When she was home three days a week, I was the one teaching her the curriculum and following what they asked me to teach. I was an organized person. We were early risers, and in the two years prior, Gracie liked to get up and get her schoolwork done—not sleep in. Not lala gag, and fight against the productive gene—shocker: she was like my husband and me.

Bringing Petrie's Story to Life

It was almost Thanksgiving again, and I wanted to focus on something other than 2nd grade during the winter. I had become Gracie's full-time manager, sometimes feeling like her assistant, leading her life and spending my time teaching her, guiding her, playing with her, and taking her on all her outings. The only thing I had going for my personal heart passions aside from getting to raise a human was cooking, cleaning, decorating, and still working on our property.

I had a tug one day and remembered that I had written about Petrie. She was now 14 years old and doing just okay. In the wee hours of the morning, I started working with an editor and illustrator. I would get up and put in a couple of hours before it was time to put on my teacher hat and head to our classroom. I didn't want it to interfere with Gracie's schedule, but the books had gained momentum. I couldn't look away. If I started the day tired, within 30 minutes I was wired—so pumped and excited about this thing I had created. Again, I believe I was tapping into the divine, and it was providing me with all the energy I needed.

It happened. Three years after they were written, I had six actual books in hand and surprised my parents. By now, you know I love to surprise them; they react in the most fabulous ways. They were stunned. My husband surprised me with a party to share with my friends and celebrate together. I decided at the time to self-publish because I wanted Petrie to look the way I saw her. They were my heart books.

Petrie passed away one month before I released them in February, the month of Valentine's Day. I waited until then because I wanted to wrap her story in the entire month of love. She was a piece of my heart, and I still cry a few times a year when I call on her and a couple of horses to play in memories together. You can find her books on my website as a tool for beginners to facilitate deeper conversations with little ones. There are six different books, including one on love, sadness, anger, jealousy, fear, and nerves.

Once the books were published, I had another desire to create the next level of emotional well-being for kids, so I constructed "Petrie's Power Up Program." I did it. I couldn't believe it. "Mrs. not technical" had figured it all out, had done it step by step herself, or had hired someone to help me with just a few pieces.

At that time, I nodded and said, "Oh, I get it, God wanted me to help kids; that was what was on my heart." Yet the Divine must've been thinking, "Aw, this is cute, let's let her do this, and then we'll get to the meat and potatoes we keep trying to tell her about." I am sure they think I am a dense human and need repeated guidance on what they are trying to tell me.

I settled in as the books and program went live, feeling really proud and relieved that I had done what the Divine had asked of me. I took a deep breath, filling my success, and heard the whisper, "You need to help women." "What! It was back." I thought I had accomplished it, and yet the foghorn started blowing in the mist, getting closer but still not actually seeing this boat, the one I was supposed to climb aboard and sail to another land.

The Lesson

Now that I was no longer pouring out my power by people-pleasing, I could hear the calling I was meant for. You're not crazy, my dear. Are you hearing a whisper or possibly a ship's horn as it blares right at you, telling you what to do? I did, and I kept being swept back into the reality of tasks that filled my day, putting it off. I took one baby step at a time, and that was okay because it was leading me slowly down to another path I was to jump upon.

When I saw the numbers appearing and heard the faint whispers and the all-knowing deep in my heart, I still didn't think it was for me. "Oops," I thought, "the divine dialed the wrong number." "That's okay, you can hang up and dial the correct person," I would state, feeling as though I wasn't qualified. I didn't think I was a leader. I didn't see myself in that way. I was an average girl fighting the good fight of trying to live a small life, a not-be-seen life, especially on social media, where more people could tell me I was wrong and not worthy.

Yet I was intrigued, peeking in, thinking, "could it be for me?" So I followed the breadcrumbs because I couldn't un-hear the whispers, and it opened up a world full of possibilities when I trusted the Divine. I couldn't see it like the faint call of the foghorn, but I could feel it, and that, my love, is pure faith.

Reflection Questions

The Divine speaks in whispers, and it takes courage to listen when we don't feel qualified to answer the call. People pleasers are the worst at answering the call because they don't know the power to pick up is within them.

1. **Have you heard a calling in your heart, a desire to step in a direction that seems huge?** Even the smallest step seems huge. You can't imagine where and when you would fit it in, or you can't afford what you are being called to. Could you break it down into tiny microsteps and take one mini-step toward the whisper? We can't always see the next move, but I believe you could take one little step.

2. **Have you been stuck thinking someone else won't "allow" you to do something, and they make you "feel" a certain way?** Let me tell you, they can't make you feel that way if that feeling isn't already inside of you. Where do you need to "allow" yourself to do something and stop blaming others?

CHAPTER 31
A FUTURE MEMORY

This is the chapter where the whispers became roars.

For years, I had been hearing faint calls—a siren song pulling me toward something I couldn't name. But I was too busy, too distracted, too focused on everyone else's needs to listen.

That was about to change.

The Sacred Bath Ritual

I was in a full-fledged zone of homeschooling, mothering, wifing, and property management. I had created an entire emotional intelligence portal for children through my books and course. I was enjoying delving into profound concepts and mental work, primarily in my weekly, blazing hot bath lit by candles and filled with bubbles. I never took baths; I only showered for most of my life, until Scott was on his second deployment, leaving me alone to fill my long, lonely weekends. During those days, I would take my time, cleaning, grocery shopping, hanging out with my grandma, who lived in California, and taking baths.

The moment I took one and read a magazine, I realized not only was it a good way to kill some time and move the following week closer to when my loved one would get to come home from Iraq, but also that it was so relaxing. I didn't stop. It became a weekly ritual that I have now maintained for 19 years, except during pregnancy. They didn't want me to scorch my baby, and I didn't want to take a "lukewarm" bath that wouldn't make my skin turn red like I had a horrid sunburn. That's the kind I enjoy. After the baby, once I got the clear, I returned to the magic of this cleansing water ritual.

When we moved home to the country and bought the house, we would spend years making our own. It had a few things that were absolute gold: a view, three rail fencing, privacy, large windows filled with dancing light, and a claw-foot tub. I had sat my tush in many baths during all our moves, mainly just the shower tub. I would scrub like the dickens before each bath, because I am a bit of a germ freak. The one tub I would never sit my tush in was the infested college apartment; my bath rituals suffered at that time.

When I sit in a steaming hot bath, my entire soul melts. I indulge in it for two hours and feel as though only thirty minutes have passed. I read, pray, and listen to music. Sometimes, I devour books. It is divine. I release some water an hour in and re-ignite the heat to get the most out of this healing practice. Not everyone loves baths, but for me, they unshackle my soul and purify my thoughts, immersing me in the next week ahead. I couldn't believe, with all the work we had to do on this place, that the divine knew the one thing I would need and could start right away on was my baths.

The Spiritual Awakening

I was content with the children's emotional support realm. I would go on to learn how to create social media posts, still something I lacked finesse in, and to promote my children's ascension work. Over the next couple of months, I saw many similar numbers. 11:11 still came and went, but others started showing up in large quantities, repeatedly. Listen, I was first in the Catholic church, then moved to the Baptist church, and now attend a nondenominational church, but we slowed down after COVID. I am a deeply spiritual being, and I could feel the connection to source energy deepening, quickening, and becoming more frequent.

I thought I was bad, listening to things that most religious people would say isn't good. I felt I was too woo-woo for religion and too religious for the woo-woo groups. I started to realize that my soul loves everyone and everything, and that I can see the connection to source energy across all religious systems and beliefs. I wasn't persuaded by either. I didn't see one wrong or right. I could see them all with the same purpose: connection, love, a deep relationship with God—the source—and the universe. Whatever you call it, as long as you aren't worshipping evil in my mind, it was all interconnected, and I love every single one. I don't feel as though I belong entirely in either group, but rather I am connected and have a deep relationship with what I call God.

I know, this might erupt your heart, but this is my journey, my story, and my soul. I don't need to be like you, and you don't need to be like me. We don't have to be so damn politically correct, creating the same life as one another, so that we can feel comfortable and safe. There is so much collectivism in this world right now that if you don't have the same perspective or opinion, especially in religion or politics, then you are wrong. You are not wrong unless you are trying to take a life, it's not yours to take. It's all interwoven, interconnected, and divine.

We get so triggered when others don't believe what we believe. Our instinct is to judge, condemn, and convince.

I watch politics rage wars inside families—people who love each other, torn apart because they don't think the same way. It baffles me.

Here's what I see instead: I see your soul. I know that every single one of us arrived here the same way—naked, screaming, birthed from a womb. We have all walked different paths since then. Different lessons. Different relationships. Different experiences with the divine. Of course, we don't all believe the same things.

But underneath it all? We are connected to the same inner knowing. The same quiet voice that guides us if we're willing to listen.

I hold everyone up. I call them forward to find their own truth—the truth that ignites their soul, that feels like coming home. Not my truth. Theirs.

I will not condemn you for your beliefs. And you cannot condemn me for mine—because I won't accept it. You can have your opinion. I'll receive the love underneath it and let it confirm who I am.

And if you're reading this feeling triggered—if someone else's opinion makes your chest tight and your defenses rise—I see you. That's your nervous system telling you you're unsafe. That's the people-pleaser inside, throwing an untamed tantrum because someone dared to disagree.

She needs healing. I know, because mine did too.

I am a reborn woman. A divinely guided soul who went from people-pleaser to purifier—purifying my own beliefs, thoughts, actions, and feelings first. And now? That healing pours out to others with ease and delight.

The Calling Becomes Clear

It hit hard again last fall. My transmutation period seems to be in the fall. I knew—I received the inner guidance—that I wanted to be a life coach for women and moms. That's where the women's piece fits so naturally. It lined up in so many ways. The thought of going back to brick-and-mortar after Gracie someday went to college and having to request a couple of weeks off to visit her seemed unacceptable. I wanted freedom. I had been spoiled by freedom as a homeschool mom, even though that meant I had many responsibilities. I couldn't imagine having a boss telling me I'd taken too much time off, and now I couldn't do what I wanted with my family or visit Gracie in college someday. So that was even more reason for this desire for life coaching to line up.

I would start slowly with my 2% of time right now, build my business, and, by the time Gracie is off on her own, I hope to have a thriving business. I have entrepreneurial generations deep in my lineage, and this all felt like that next step I was being called toward. I would think about it, and divine numbers would start calling me in. I would raise questions and doubts in my brain, and the numbers would arrive. I started looking them up as this was happening, and I would scream with delight at each confirmation. It was guidance, guidance from something larger than me.

The Decision

My husband was on a trip to his company's once-a-year event, again. He's actually home a lot; however, I have many revelations when I lie quietly in bed, not snuggling in his cocoon of warmth. When he called me that evening, I had already decided. I decided that amid this busy time in my life and while already being the rightful owner of two previous full-fledged careers, I was coming to the mothership. I wanted it, I could see it, I felt it. It felt like home, it felt like alignment with the direction I had already poured a few years of work into. I was naturally a great listener and empathizer. I needed the structure to guide or, really, the certification to feel qualified. Yep, that was still slightly there.

I told him on the phone what it would cost and what it would take for the next eight months for a dual certification. The certainty in my voice wasn't telling him I would do it, but it wasn't asking permission either. We combined all our finances when we got married, and out of respect for each other, we chat with the other person for anything over a certain amount. He said, "Okay, go for it." I thought for sure he would fight me on it. We were on one income, and I had already spent extra on this passion project adventure path I was going down. I screamed in delight, walking on our gravel road, and the horses picked up their head and looked in my direction. I enrolled that night, and the new program started the following week.

The Lesson

I wasn't wobbly. I didn't go to my hubby with questions when I was still unsure—he would have gone against it, knowing my energy didn't fully support it. I was back in my zone and ascending to new heights. People-pleasing was becoming a rearview memory. I had learned to say no in all the groups with the other moms. Even with my close family, whom I cared about so deeply, I was starting to learn, as a former people pleaser, how to say yes to myself, how to desire something and hold the pose, with a deep knowing like a future memory that I had seen that it was just going to happen. This wasn't about forcing the other person to do something. This was about choosing something that lit me up and then standing in patient conviction while I explained it.

Reflection Questions

When we honestly claim our desires with unwavering certainty, God and the universe conspire to make them happen.

1. **Where, my love, are you shaky in your asking?** As a people pleaser, you have to shift into a confident knowing; otherwise, the other person will question if you actually desire it.

2. **Is it a piece of you, like a future memory you have already seen?** Can you feel it as if it's already yours? What does it look like? Who are you when you are doing it?

3. **What would it look like to claim it with certainty?** How would you ask for what you need? What are the words that you need to speak?

CHAPTER 32
GENERATIONAL SHIFTS

This chapter broke my heart—and then it rebuilt it stronger.

I had done the work. I had broken free. But when I looked at my daughter, I saw it: the people-pleaser traits had already been passed down. She was apologizing for everything. Asking permission for things that didn't need permission.

The patterns I had fought so hard to break were already taking root in her.

But here's what I learned: it's not too late. Generational healing works forward AND backward. And I was about to prove it.

Stepping Into My Purpose

I committed to learning all they had to teach in the life and health coaching classes. I devoured the morsels I needed and paired them with personal experiences I learned along the way. I invested in a couple of other courses that were calling to me and would help me embody the next step. I was stepping weekly toward the upleveled version of myself.

I had the pleasure of raising a girl with a heart of gold, a strong work ethic, confidence, and kindness that seemed to radiate from her like the sun, warming anyone who crossed her path. I was starting to feed her with the information I had learned over the years, and she welcomed my elevated, inquisitive, and deep conversations. As I became clearer, stepping on new paths one after the other, I started to see what had formed, and I was sadly appalled. Many generations and my own previous unhealed energy had come down and begun to create a people-pleaser within her.

I cringed, knowing I was part of that lineage. I had seen it clearly when my mom's old habit would rear its ugly head, and she would lovingly correct Gracie and show her how to hold other people's feelings above her own. It is up to us to choose another way consciously. This tactic is so apparent to me now that I have done so much inner work around it, and fortunately, I can spot it right away. I had conversations with my mom several years back, letting her know it wasn't serving its purpose the way she lovingly thought it was. Because I recognize it so quickly now, it no longer happens. She was so immersed in it that she couldn't escape it. She honestly didn't realize it was happening, like putting on an old, worn-out, hole-ridden shirt because it's comfy, although you're not actually sure it fits you anymore.

I had been able to stop that train between Gracie and my mom and rebuild Gracie's ability to acknowledge her feelings, thoughts, and concerns. My mom is learning to do the same. She is setting her own boundaries and has become a freer soul in doing so. Whenever my mom and I indulged in girl time, I poured out my heart and lifted my mom into this new dimension with me. She is always curious about what I am up to. She still loves, to this day, having deep conversations that blow her mind, and I am sure she walks away thinking I am cuckoo for Cocoa Puffs.

The Ache of Recognition

Seeing the people-pleasing traits in my daughter gutted me.

The shame tried to swallow me whole. How could I let this happen? How could I pass down the very chains I was fighting to break?

But I caught myself. The shame was the old programming—telling me I had failed, that it was too late, that the damage was done.

It wasn't too late. The damage could be healed. And I was the one who would heal it.

Gracie was five by the time I started cracking open the vault and escaping this people-pleasing prison; she had already been affected. I could see it coursing through her blood and behavior. She was radiant, confident, and bold when she was sure the other person loved her. I've received hundreds of compliments on the human being she is, and on how her soul interacts with others, yet at the same time, she was apologizing for everything and asking permission to do silly things like get a drink. What happened?

From the outside, it would look like we beat her, and the fridge is locked at home. She was dripping with people-pleasing apologies and requests for permission, just trying to get through the day. We could see it slowly growing, but once I had healed those pieces of me, hers stood out like a sore thumb, making my mothering heart ache with failure. I had caught it in myself and was guiding and helping her slowly ascend into a healthy emotional and mental space. I now had a hold of Gracie and my mother, who had both been affected by generational patterns, and together, I would help heal generations forward and backward.

There was a loud voice echoing, telling me I failed, that I hadn't gotten to it in time, and that I had done the same thing my mother had, which left me in disarray. I had done the thing that pained me for so long. I didn't do it in the same way, but I didn't have the tools to fix it until now. I knew I didn't like it, and I was on the way to the store to get the tools, but her damage had been done. The damage is less than what I carried. The way it happened was through witnessing how I behaved, not because I didn't validate her, spend time with her, listen to her, and witness her. She and I are close—so beautifully close. She is my mini-me, and she picked up my bad habits along with everything else.

Divine Timing

As I became aware of the storm swirling within her, a beautiful spiritual thing began to happen. I would learn something profound, something that would alter my perspective so deeply I couldn't unsee it. The next thing I knew, Gracie would ask a question that applied to that exact teaching, a complex question that I would have struggled with in my past or doubted myself in not having the correct answer to build her up and help her release the chains. She has stopped me in my tracks a few times because I have just embodied something, and she brings it up on the same day. I get to invite her up with me.

It is so interconnected and beautiful. She has no idea about the squirrel paths I go down or what I study, yet she then asks me something I just learned. This is pure Divine timing. It is the Divine that not only helps me teach her but also affirms in me that this is so important. It lights me up knowing I am getting to pour pure gold into this little being as she steps into her teenage years.

I am in awe that this is my life—the one I have created, the one I dreamt of, and the one I had to keep stepping toward my desires and my heart's path. I know all too well the woman who sacrifices, who works her ass off, who gives more and more out of fear of not being understood, loved, or connected with. It took me 30+ years to start putting it all together, and as the pieces clicked into place, it was obvious: no one could choose me, lift me, understand me, connect to me, and love me if I couldn't do it for myself.

I am in the deepest, most supportive, and most loving relationship I have ever had with myself and my loved ones. The relationships around me are upleveling to become my best match. It is a divine, pleasurable, orgasmic feeling. I feel high on life every single day, and my daughter, my mother, and many generations, both forward and backward, are healing.

The Healing Journey

If you recall from earlier in my story, I wasn't sure whether I was worthy of being a mom at all, let alone being a stay-at-home mom who didn't earn money and therefore, in my mind, didn't feel adequate. This has been a ride, the ride of my life. I look back and see how I was growing and expanding all those years, when my nervous system told me I needed to work to have value. I breathed into the pain and discomfort. I faced the daily grind and joy of cleaning the house five times a day, chasing a toddler, and having lather, rinse, repeat on what felt like Groundhog Day as I raised a child at home alone.

Despite all those items that typically make people go bonkers and return to work, I found magic in raising the most important thing on earth, a soul that was given to me. When I reflect, I can now see that because I did the hard thing and didn't give up the good fight, I was able to heal. This was the healing. Every chance I got, I delved into another thought, another pattern, or another idea that would alter my perspective.

Having Gracie and staying at home with her healed me. It went against the generations and the collective thinking that was being thrown at me so heavily. I had to hold the freaking pose, even when friends and family members were dropping like flies and going back to the grind of work because they literally said they had to "use their brains again." Instead, I picked up the next deep-thinking book, dreamed about the what-ifs, spent so much time playing and giggling with my precious girl, nurtured my husband, grew beautiful plants, and dove into any deep topic that called to me. And after five years of that, I wrote children's books, I created a website and programs to help others heal, and now I am releasing this book.

Motherhood fucking healed me because I let it, and I look that little soul, Gracie, in the eyes and I tell her profound, heartfelt thank-you's for choosing me.

The Lesson

If you feel called to change things in yourself and in your children's lives, don't settle. Raise the bar and your vibration. Take the humble path to see how you could do it better—not in a people-pleaser way, but in a take-charge-of-future-generations way.

If you feel guilty about something you've done, forgive yourself, shift, and move forward. I couldn't go back and change who I was in the first five to seven years of Gracie's life, but I could show her what's possible. The people pleaser had almost vanished from my life, and I didn't loop or send myself into despair for what I saw. I wanted her to see that at any point in your life, you can shift your mental awareness and choose differently. I wanted her to know she doesn't have to buy into society's idea of what a mom should do to be accepted by the world. I wanted her to see a different path—a path where she can be at home with her babies, pouring nourishment and love into them, all while having something creative and powerful to build on the side if she chooses. I wanted her to have an example of what's possible: a loving marriage, a deep connection with her kids, a beautiful home, and a passion project that lights up her soul and heals others. She gets to have it all and so much more.

One more thing: being a people pleaser is exhausting. I have moderated what I say time and time again, not from intentional manipulation but from fear of hurting the other person. It takes enormous energy to listen while simultaneously calculating the perfect response. When you heal the people pleaser, this is released. You're no longer performing—you're an active participant in the current moment. You'll have so much more energy when you aren't trying to stay three steps ahead to make sure your best foot is forward. You will be more relaxed, joyful, compassionate, open, and discerning. It is SO worth it.

Reflection Questions

Generational patterns don't have to define your future—you have the power to heal forward and backward.

1. **What generational habit are you carrying like a bag of coal, heavy and leaving soot everywhere?** What did you swear you'd never do, yet find yourself repeating?

2. If you have the awareness that something needs to change, you're meant to change it. **What's one step you can take today?** Have a conversation with your loved ones to get everyone on the same page. If they don't support you yet but you still feel called, you're most likely meant to show them the way.

3. It might feel like standing at the base of a mountain, not knowing how you'll ever reach the top. But it only takes one step at a time, my love. **How does the healed version of you move, act, live, and love?** Get clear on who she is, and decide she is here now.

Untamed Bonus: For the Stay-at-Home Moms

If you're a stay-at-home mom struggling to stay the course, you are seen, felt, heard, and so loved. I know you clean multiple times a day, listen to kid songs ten thousand times over, and wonder if anyone is having adult conversations. In those moments at home, instead of cleaning for the tenth time while baby naps, pick up a book, do a workout, feed your mind, take a bath, nourish yourself somehow. Make it your non-negotiable.

If you really hate staying home—if you've read the books and done everything you can think of to bring yourself joy, yet you're yelling, disconnected, and not engaging well with your kids—get help. Try going back to work part-time and see if that's enough. If not, go full-time. But don't go back because society thinks you should do it all, or because you're bored. There are ten million things to do in this world, and many don't cost money. Ask yourself what you could build from home and pursue a passion you've always had.

Let me be very clear: I am not shaming moms who work full-time. Many working moms would kill to stay home. My heart wants to hug you. I see your deep longing to witness every giggle, step, and tear. You are seen, heard, and loved for providing your little ones with the life you desire for them.

I understand not everyone can live off one salary, but my husband made $49,000 a year when we decided to keep me home. We enjoyed finding ways to have fun for free or at low cost. We purchased quality used vehicles and didn't "keep up with the Joneses." We focused on our goals, knowing that someday I would work again, but I wouldn't be able to rewind time to be at home with Gracie and witness her childhood.

If you've been longing to stay at home and your spouse supports it, but you're worried about spending, make a budget. Lay out all your expenses and see where you're overspending on items that don't even bring you joy. Find a way to cut corners and fill your soul with meaning instead of shopping. There will be a time you can do all that again—maybe sooner than you think, as you build a fierce business from home.

Whatever you choose, choose it because it's what you know deep down to be the path you're being led to—not because the limiting beliefs in your head are winning.

CHAPTER 33
UNLEASHING THE SIREN

This is it. The chapter where everything came together—and the woman I was born to be finally stood up and claimed her place.

The people-pleaser who had run my life for 40+ years? She's dead. Not dying. Not fading. DEAD.

And in her place? A woman on fire with purpose, untamed, unstoppable, pouring out power from an overflow that never runs dry.

This is how it happened.

Vibrational Bliss

I had now created a 12-week women's program, "Vibrational Bliss," to help you remember you have a body attached to that fierce, workaholic, badass, disconnected head of yours. I take you deep into small steps of learning how to step back into your feminine and out of the masculine that is running the show, creating burnout because you don't have the testosterone of a man, whether it's your own or bioidentical. I guide you on how to start seeing your feminine flow become pleasure-filled and held by the masculine container within you. I worked on it as it flowed from my now-embodied self.

I nurtured Gracie in it as she began to step into pre-teenhood, learning to love herself deeply and not always needing permission. We are still on that journey as we have just started at the time I write this book, but her breakthroughs are profound and magnetic. She is beautiful to witness. When I send her to other houses, or we meet someone new, I never think about correcting what she says, and she is wonderfully respectful of those around her. She is deeply committed to her core beliefs and willing to be open-minded, even when the topic is unusual.

The Trainer's Concern

Last summer, she spent time with an old family friend she sees once a week for a lesson. This adult is passionate, caring, loving, strong, and an excellent role model for young ladies. She is firm and matter-of-fact, and has had a profound impact on both Gracie and my life. I wouldn't trade it for the world; she has been a godsend in our journey. Gracie had a camp session with this adult and some of her friends, who are all good kiddos with their own unique flair, paths, and convictions. They differ in how they interact.

The trainer who hosted the camp called me a few days later, concerned because Gracie had asked for permission to go outside and check on her horse. None of the other girls had asked permission; they just did it, not all at the same time, but bit by bit. She also explained that she thought my being at horse shows put a lot of pressure on Gracie, even though she had never witnessed me say anything negative to Gracie at those shows. She just thought my presence might set high expectations for Gracie. I listened to this long-time friend express her concerns and told her I would discuss it with my family.

At first, I was confused. I thought to myself, she was calling to tell me that while my daughter was staying at her house and on her schedule, Gracie behaved respectfully, asked if it was a good time to check on her horse, and also let the trainer know where she would be. In my adult mind, I took that to be responsible and respectful of someone else's time and home. The trainer took it as a sign that Gracie needed more confidence. Interesting—I thought—so the child who was showing manners and respect to an adult was being questioned.

I was reminded later that she had spent many years handling teenage girls, including me, and all the glory that came with it—strong-willed teenagers who are ready to fire back or do as they please, and to apologize later if caught. She is a saint, an absolute treasure to the teenage girls who are impacted and influenced by her. I will forever be grateful that she entered my life and became part of our family. It's odd for a child to respond the way Gracie does, and I listened to the trainer's concern about boosting a child's confidence.

I didn't panic and thought, "Oh my gosh, this woman is telling me I am a bad mom—what have I done?" Which, yes, several years prior, would have been my response as the people-pleaser. I held it, examined it, and assessed it. I appreciated being reminded of another perspective from an outsider and how it must look. I spoke with Gracie and my husband that night, and everything this trainer had said had Gracie baffled. She loved having me close at shows. I wiped off her boots, held her water, brought her snacks, and helped her understand a pattern. We paid this trainer to help her with patterns. Still, Gracie has a laser-like memory that has been building for nearly five years now, through all her music practice, allowing her to memorize songs to play on the guitar and sing, which in turn helps her remember equestrian patterns easily.

Gracie was also met with the realization that this trainer was assisting her competition, and she wasn't always available when Gracie had a question, so what looked like pressure from the outside was me, hanging out, boosting her up, and even cheering her on with joy if the class didn't go so great. I was relieved to hear that was how she was experiencing me, and I trust she told me the truth, given our years of talking, and even my genuine question once a year about how I could support her in being a better mom. Yes, I listen to what this little soul needs, and I adjust, even if my ego wants to take over.

I didn't reply to the trainer right away, as a people pleaser would want to fix it as soon as possible; I let it just be. It became a beautiful unfolding while on the phone when I gave the trainer an example of how strong, confident, independent, convicted, and committed Gracie is toward the people she spends a lot of time with. She is a gorgeous amalgamation of grit and grace. She shares her truth and her thoughts, even if they are hard to hear, and wraps it all up in a blanket of respect. She knows who she is, what she doesn't like, and responds immediately, but you must be around her enough and listen; then she will let her power soar. Her confidence is seen by most around her and perceived differently by each person. She will not be like everyone else, and she doesn't care. She is still growing. We are still unraveling the people-pleaser within her. But I KNOW it's working.

When she looks at another teen trying to pressure her and says, "I don't respond to peer pressure"—that's the new programming taking hold.

When she shares her truth, even when it's hard to hear—that's the generational chain breaking.

I didn't save her from being affected at all. But I caught it in time to teach her how to break free. And that? That's everything.

 I know she is powerful, especially when she responds to other teens trying to pressure her with the exact words, "I don't respond to peer pressure."

My husband and I screamed and laughed out loud when she told us that is how she handled a situation with another teen. "Hell yes, girl, fix that crown, spread those wings and soar, my love, you are so damn cool!"

The Calling Becomes Clear

After I released my first women's program, I saw how God was bringing together all my past experiences and personal learnings, providing a place for me not only to support children but also to support mothers, empowering and purifying the delicate hearts together. I saw how intertwined it became. Yet I was still wondering what the specific thing I wanted to teach was. I am not speaking of a niche—I couldn't narrow it down. I am feminine; the feminine is multi-faceted and multi-passionate. So far, I have been in three different careers, but this one feels like coming home.

There it was again, another feeling of something brewing, but I couldn't place my finger on it. The only thing I felt and sensed was the word "healing," which wasn't very clear and could go in many ways. I was now flirting with the numbers that were coming my way again. Over the last year, nature has started interacting with me more, and wild animals have begun approaching me, specifically one in particular who would often come back again and again. I would pray about something or be chewing on an idea. It would appear, not just in the distance but right in front of me, multiple times. If I were driving and didn't see it, my daughter would point it out. She also did this with numbers; she had no idea I took them seriously. I believe my guides were coming through her to convey and do things that I was seeking answers to.

The Conference

It was May, and school was ending. I had desired to attend a women's conference somewhere, but I wanted to find the right one, as I was in a different realm than some I had previously attended, and I wanted to feel alive and inspired in all my hippie, cowgirl, woo-woo ways. I had searched for a couple of months, but nothing really snagged my heart. Since I wasn't going to spend money on that, we decided to go on a family vacation to a place I had always wanted to visit but hadn't yet been to: Florida. I investigated it. I found a place where we could swim with the dolphins.

Gracie and I squealed as we ran all over the house that day. There were two months ahead to dream about what that would be like. We also booked a trip to the Everglades, making really unique memories and creating an unforgettable experience.

A few weeks after I booked our Florida fun vacation, a woman I had been following posted a video that was then removed shortly after. She had let her followers know about an up-leveled women's conference taking place in my home state. I was flabbergasted. This is what I have been waiting for. I found myself saying it was too much. I have already booked a vacation, and now I want to attend a conference by myself. I heard the thoughts. I felt the pull back into staying safe and not pushing the limits I apparently set for myself: I can only take one fun vacation a year.

A louder voice appeared. It felt like it was in the depths of my body, and I couldn't let it go. I was out running errands and texted my husband that I had finally found the women's conference I was looking for and would love to attend; however, it costs an xyz amount. I decided to say it and put it out there, as the pull was stronger than the desire to stay small. I thought, "It's okay if he says no; at least I tried." He replied, "Book it." I screamed because that's what I do now. Are you kidding? Could I attend this conference on my own, stay at the gorgeous hotel where a room has been blocked, and treat myself? I paused, and then, "Yes, I can!"

The only thing holding me back was myself, because I was playing small. I wasn't imagining I could take a beautiful trip to Florida and then spend a few days recharging and powering up at a conference, all for the sake of paying it forward to you. It was my block, and if I believed in that block, I would continue to see evidence of it.

The Awakening

I went to the conference.

And I walked out a completely different woman.

Everything I had been working on for years—YEARS—got activated. Embodied. Locked in. The whispers I had been hearing became a roar I couldn't ignore. The purpose I had been circling finally came into focus so clearly that I couldn't unsee it.

The people-pleaser didn't die quietly. She clawed and begged and whispered lies until the very end. But she is dead now.

I stepped so far outside my reality that I had no option but to change. Everything I had been working on for years—yes, years—got embodied and locked in by going. It awakened things in me that I had long forgotten or had seen as memories in the future. The conference was powerful, but the work I had previously done needed to be activated. This activation occurred because I stepped outside my usual existence to be immersed in a massive energy environment. Years of forgotten truths that came with my soul flooded in, and the past 10 years of breaking free from people-pleasing were entrusted to me—to teach you.

When it was over, I left the gorgeous downtown hotel room that held me like a cozy comfort after being in such high energy all day. I left feeling so held, heart wide open, and different. I felt relaxed, as during the whole conference I stayed very present and didn't let my brain take over, getting overwhelmed by the large number of people and their own energies. I traveled by Uber for 45 minutes in silence, processing what I had taken in. He took me to a hotel closer to the airport, in the middle of a field that was still being developed. I walked across the room, sat on the edge of the bed, and looked out at the vast land with long, yellowed grass.

A feeling of pressure and heavy energy literally melted from my head like a deep sigh of breath being released all the way down through my feet and out of my body. I am energy-sensitive, but I had never felt this sensation so intensely in such a quiet space. I thought about it, and I realized it was because I had escaped the hustle and bustle of the busy city, and this country girl could finally relax and release all the energy I was holding as I looked out at the vast open field. I giggled to myself and said, "Wow, I need wide open spaces apparently," and I still think that was a portion of the release. However, I now see it as a release of what I had carried for 41 years of my life, finally letting go, because the next day on the plane ride home, I would create the outline of this book and its program to follow.

I am so convicted of what my soul is here to do; it was so clear I couldn't unsee it. The energy was untamable, like a wild stampede of horses. I didn't care what was in my way. I would be forever changed, so changed that I have now written this entire book in three weeks. It's pouring out of me. It's the core of who I am here to be and how I am to help contribute to the world through the lessons my soul was meant to learn. I know how to deeply guide you like a "siren" in the breeze, beckoning you to your own sovereign soul, asking you to listen to the whispers that are calling you inward, begging you to free yourself from the shackles, chains and pens that are keeping you from seeing what your soul actually wants to do—taking you from people-pleasing to unlatching the gate, instead of pouring out your power—you are set free to run, Untamed.

She no longer explains herself—her boundaries are invisibly enforced.

She no longer manages reactions—she knows they don't belong to her.

She no longer survives on approval—she IS her own approval.

She no longer adjusts to be accepted—she adjusts to fit what's right for HER.

She no longer hides in the corner—she engages when desired.

She no longer questions everything she speaks—she releases words that are aligned.

The woman I was—the one who dimmed her light to make others comfortable—is gone.

I buried her in the dirt of every choice I made to stay small. And from that grave, something WILD grew.

I am Untamed.

Not reckless. Not selfish. Not cruel.

Just finally, fiercely, unapologetically MYSELF.

She no longer pours out her power—she runs UNTAMED, pouring from her overflow.

With Velvet and Fire,
Rachel

Untamed Bonus: The Sacred Number 33

Hi Loves, this book was meant to be known, and my fingers were the pathway. When I wrote Chapter 22, I kept hearing 33. I didn't force it to be 33 chapters; it beckoned to me and you, my love. I followed the story of my life and the messages I had for us in this book, and the last chapter was Chapter 33. So, I want you to hear the message this book is intended for you to receive.

Spiritual significance of the #33: "is a powerful master number representing divine connection, spiritual enlightenment, compassion, and creativity. It is a call to personal transformation, encourages one to embrace their creative potential, and serves as a reminder to be compassionate and kind to others, aligning with one's true life's purposes."

I mean, wow—#33 wants you to be a good human as you transform into your true life purpose. My love, your life's purpose isn't to pour out your power, lighting the path because you are a servant of others, but rather, to pour out your gold from your radiant, abundant, loving, nurturing, badass overflow, and not even be able to stop the way you light up the world around you.

Don't spend another day pouring out your gold without first filling your cup. It all works that way, and you will power up the world with much more spiritual love if you put your mask on first before assisting others, just like they say on the airplanes.

Get it, my love. Do the work. Light up your soul. Find your "Hell Yes's," and then power up your world around you with your special, magnetic offering and magnificent glow!

Unlacing your journey,

Rachel

BONUS: A MASCULINE PERSPECTIVE

Watching Her Rise

I married a woman who once kept the peace at her own expense.

She was generous and agreeable, always reading the room and adjusting accordingly. For a long time, I thought this was just kindness. I thought love meant keeping everyone happy.

But love, I've learned, requires men to be braver than that.

When a Woman Stops Hiding

A woman who has lived as a people-pleaser has often learned—consciously or not—that love is maintained through self-erasure. She keeps things running smoothly by suppressing her own needs so no one else feels uncomfortable.

When she begins to heal, the first thing that changes isn't her love. It's her silence.

She pauses before answering. She says no without a lengthy explanation. She stops shrinking.

As a husband, this can feel unsettling. The familiar peace disappears. But what replaces it is something deeper: who she truly is.

Reflection: Truth doesn't destroy intimacy—it creates the possibility for more of it.

What Happened Inside Me

Before I could respond well to her transformation, I had to face what it stirred up in me. When my wife's confidence began to surface, it awakened fears I didn't know I carried:

- Am I failing her?
- Why is she changing our routine?
- Is this my fault?
- Am I losing my family?

These questions didn't come from logic. They came from fear.

My instinct was to fix her, correct the situation, or distance myself emotionally so I wouldn't have to feel uncomfortable. I've done all of these. And I can tell you plainly—none of it is leadership.

What Leadership Actually Looks Like

Control is often mistaken for strength. Many of us were taught that leadership means having answers, directing outcomes, or restoring calm as fast as possible.

But authentic leadership is different.

A leading man doesn't rush to resolve tension. He doesn't flee discomfort. He stays steady in the space—even when words come out imperfectly, even when clarity hasn't arrived yet.

This is strength, not control, and not running away trying to escape. The quiet power of staying present while she unfolds.

This kind of presence tells her, you are safe here, you are not too much, we will figure this out together.

Reflection: Before difficult conversations, pause. Ask yourself: Can I stay open without defending my position? Do I need a moment before I respond?

When hard conversations come—about needs, boundaries, family history, long-held hurts—your presence matters more than your answers.

A man offering a shoulder does three things:

1. **He stays present** — No withdrawing, shutting down, or sarcasm.
2. **He listens without correcting** — Her experience doesn't need to be fixed.
3. **He reassures simply** — "I'm here." "We'll work through this together."

Men—this is our time to step up. Be her strength without controlling the conversation. Your presence in the room matters more than you realize.

Reflection: When emotions rise, do I become a wall—or a safe place to land?

A Word to Women: How to Invite Him In

Men often hear emotional change as a problem to solve. The way you communicate your growth can determine whether he leans in or shuts down.

Phrases that help:

- "This is something I'm learning about myself."
- "This boundary is about me—it doesn't mean you failed."
- "I don't need you to fix this. I need you to hear me."
- "I want us to walk through this together."

Blame triggers defense. An invitation creates a connection.

Reflection: Words spoken with care generate a connection. Words spoken with contempt spark disconnection.

What This Journey Gave Us

My wife's confidence didn't diminish our marriage. It strengthened it. Her voice asked more of me. I became more present. More intentional. More honest about my own limits and fears.

I am no longer married to a woman who disappears to keep the peace. I am married to a woman who stands for what she believes in.

My advice to men: Don't shrink her courage. Stand beside it.

Weekly Practice:

Once a week, ask your wife: "Is there anything you've been holding back that you want to share?"

Then listen. Without interruption. Without fixing.

You won't always agree. That's okay. You can respect each other anyway.

This chapter isn't an invitation to be perfect. It's an invitation to be present.

The work is ongoing. The reward is a marriage where neither of you has to disappear.

— Scott Piccoli

CONTINUE THE JOURNEY

If this book stirred something in you—if you felt seen, if you recognized yourself in these pages, if something inside you whispered "I'm ready"—I want you to know: this doesn't have to end here.

I created a program called **Untamed Velvet** for women who are done reading about transformation and ready to live it.

Here's what I want you to understand first:

You were not born a people-pleaser. This was learned. Conditioned. Absorbed from the world around you as you tried to feel safe and loved. You are not broken. You do not need to carry shame for patterns that were never yours to begin with.

But now you know. And knowing means you get to choose.

Untamed Velvet is a deep dive into:

- Where your people-pleaser came from
- Which type shows up in your life
- The fear or shame driving her
- The hidden programs keeping her alive
- And how to finally, fully break free

It's a blend of masculine logic and feminine body and spiritual work—because healing isn't just about understanding. It's about embodying.

If you're curious, visit **Hummingblissacres.com** and flirt with the idea that you could finally be set free.

No pressure. Just an open door.

I'll be on the other side if you decide to walk through.

With Velvet and Fire, Rachel